Novel Ideas
for
Young Readers!

NOVEL IDEAS
FOR
YOUNG READERS!

Projects and Activities

Katherine Wiesolek Kuta

Susan Zernial, Ed.D.

2000
Teacher Ideas Press
A Division of Libraries Unlimited, Inc.
Englewood, Colorado

TEACHER IDEAS PRESS
A Division of
Libraries Unlimited, Inc.
P.O. Box 6633
Englewood, CO 80155-6633
1-800-237-6124
www.lu.com/tip

Library of Congress Cataloging-in-Publication Data

Kuta, Katherine Wiesolek, 1952-
    Novel ideas for young readers! : projects and activities / Katherine Wiesolek Kuta,
Susan C. Zernial.
        p. cm.
    ISBN 1-56308-791-X (softbound)
    1. Reading (Elementary) 2. Literature--Study and teaching (Elementary) 3.
Children--Books and reading. I. Zernial, Susan C. II. Title.

LB1573 .K85 2000
372.64'044--dc21

                                                                                00-060778

*This book is dedicated to several special readers
in my family who I am fortunate
to see read, learn, and grow constantly.*

*My enchanting daughter, Melanie, who reads and writes at age seven
and creates wonderful stories for me to listen to and enjoy daily.
She also inspires me to write more for children.*

*My godchild, Laura, who has once again become
connected with me
and makes me treasure our time together.*

*My godchild, Joey, whose imagination, humor, and creativity over
the last eleven years constantly surprise everyone.
He enriches me with his performances.*

*My niece, Karly, who has been sweet and insightful
for the last nine years
and helps me feel young at heart.*

—Katherine Wiesolek Kuta

Contents

Part II—Representing and Viewing Standards Activities (*continued*)

Part III—Speaking and Listening Standards Activities 95

Preface

This book provides activities and projects for teachers to use with their students as before-, during-, and after-reading activities with any kind of fiction. It is also possible to use some activities with nonfiction reading material. This resource book can be used as authentic assessment as well as performance assessment because all the activities involve students displaying their knowledge and understanding of a book or short story in a creative, original manner. Students can work on these projects in groups, in pairs, or as individuals as directed by the teacher.

This book offers 60 varied activities and projects to accommodate many different learning styles. Some students may prefer activities that require more reading and writing, if they are skilled in these areas. Other students may prefer creating objects that represent their knowledge, if they tend to be more "hands-on" learners. Students who are exceptionally verbal may feel most comfortable speaking to an audience for their project. Teachers should offer choice and variety to accommodate students' interests whenever possible, but all students should be exposed to all modes of expression and skills during the course of the school year.

Most of these activities can be adapted for any grade level, ability group, type of class, or type of literature. Because teachers' purposes for assigning an activity will vary, as will the skills that need reinforcing, the activities are divided into three sections with 20 activities per section. Each section emphasizes two of the six language arts standards: reading, writing, representing, viewing, speaking, listening.

Selection of the material was based on successful classroom-tested projects. I have used most of the activities with students from kindergarten through high school. As expected in good teaching, I constantly revise and adapt activities as I find out what works, especially after feedback from my students. Even though most of my experience is with high school students, I have found all students have several common needs. They need the opportunity to express themselves individually, to be successful, to increase self-esteem, and to learn about themselves and the world they live in. A way to do all of the above is through children's literature and activity projects.

Through my experiences, I have met with many professional teachers who have shared ideas with me. I have saved, changed, and molded these ideas to fit my needs and the needs of the students that I was working with at any one time. I am thankful to all my colleagues who shared ideas and materials with me when I was the "new kid on the block" during the years of starting over with a new class, grade level, or school. This book has now allowed me to organize the old as well as create the new so that I can share successful materials with others.

I have also been very fortunate to work with Susan Zernial as a consultant for this book. She has wonderful expertise as an editor and irreplaceable experience as an elementary school teacher. She has been able to simplify and look at material from an experienced, practical point of view.

I have taught remedial students during my entire teaching career, and there are three factors that I have found add to success with students. The first is to plan a variety of activities for use within a class. The second is to give students the power of choice; and the third is to use children's and young adult literature in the classroom. I wrote this book with these three factors constantly in mind.

Because teachers like ready-made materials that meet their needs, the activities and projects are reproducible. Each activity/project has a list of purposes, how to use the activity, evaluation, and variations. Teachers can change or enlarge the forms as they feel necessary.

I hope that you become more enriched with ideas by using this book with your students and that your students learn and grow to be lifelong readers.

Katherine Wiesolek Kuta

Introduction

With the publication of the International Reading Association and the National Council of Teachers of English's Standards for English/Reading Language Arts in 1996, I felt a need to show teachers the kinds of activities and projects already being done successfully in the classroom that match these standards. These six necessary skill standards—reading, writing, representing, viewing, speaking, and listening—are stated specifically in the 12 student-centered standards.

More recently in many states, there is an increasing emphasis on goals, standards, benchmarks, and performance assessment at all levels. The activities and projects in this book are geared toward performance assessment that coincides with the six basic skill areas. My editor and I feel a strong need to reach the early elementary-level students to establish the necessary connections to literature, so the goal of this book is twofold: (1) students should begin to develop the six skills and (2) students should make connections with print and form strong memory impressions thereby increasing comprehension.

I created this book as a desk reference of practical, classroom-tested ideas for teachers to use when planning units and lessons with fiction. However, some of the activities/projects can be used with nonfiction readings. Students can accomplish most of these activities in groups, in pairs, or as individuals. Students often learn from each other when put in cooperative group settings. Students need to learn to play, work, and communicate with one another at an early age to help prepare for later in life.

The first part of this book concentrates on real-life reading and writing activity projects. The projects include writing paragraphs, news stories, letters, summaries, fiction, and creative responses. These projects are grouped together because the students are involved in reading a book and also in having a writing experience concerned with the book. These activities are not in any particular order, so a teacher can choose a specific activity to meet a specific purpose or offer several activities from which students may choose.

The second part of this book deals with activities and projects that offer students the opportunity to exhibit their knowledge of a book visually, such as with a chart or artwork. In this part, the students must read a piece of literature either individually or collectively, and there may be some kind of writing involved. The focus, however, is on the information in the reading and the students' ability to make connections with and representations of that information in an unusual, creative format as requested by the activity/project. Formats include a collage, poster, mobile, mural, bumper sticker, bookmark, or greeting card.

The second phase of each project includes sharing the creation with class members. Students take responsibility for their learning by sharing with and learning from one another. This cooperation enables the teacher to act as a facilitator in the classroom. The use of visual representations becomes a teaching device for students during formal or informal presentations.

The third part of the book offers activities and projects for students to practice speaking and listening standards. The activities were designed for students to present orally to the class and also, in some instances, to be creative. Some activities are a mini booktalk, a panel discussion, an interview, an oral book review, and poems. The class members get to practice their listening skills as the audience for the presentations.

For all 60 activities, there are explanation sheets that give the teacher pertinent information on the purposes of the activities, how to use the activities, evaluation points, and variations of the activities. All activity sheets are reproducible and ready to use in the classroom. The variety in the activities makes this resource book a useful tool to increase students' participation and motivation, as well as to assess students' performance in language arts. If you decide to use an activity for performance assessment, you will need to develop an appropriate rubric to evaluate specific skills. You can mix and match any of the activities and alter them in any way necessary for individual purposes.

Part 1
Reading and Writing Standards Activities

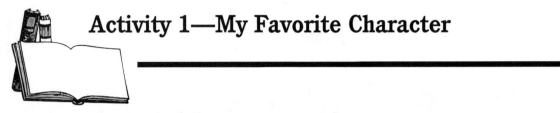

Activity 1—My Favorite Character

Purpose of the Activity

The purpose of this activity is to involve students as active readers. They will be writing and taking notes about a character as they read the book. Students will also reflect on whether they think the character is likable or not based on the information they have on the graphic organizer, which is a visual structure that displays information. Then they must write and support their choice.

How to Use the Activity

Use the form as a model for students during reading, starting at the beginning of the book. Many times the information about main characters appears during the exposition, generally in the first few pages. Depending on their age group, students can learn about exposition and character development by recording information on this form. After a degree of comfort is reached over time, this activity can be assigned to groups, pairs, or individuals.

Evaluation

The assessment of the activity could be based on participation, discussion, completion, and understanding. Hopefully, as students become more careful readers, they will automatically become aware of character description as they read. The goal is for the students to move toward independence.

Variations

For concrete learners, students could be asked to draw the character based on the description or cut out a picture from a magazine. For the personality traits, students could be asked to draw or create symbols. For the other information, students could be asked to place words or phrases around their drawing.

Activity 1—My Favorite Character

Name: _____ Date:_____

Title: _____

Author: _____

Publisher and year: _____

Directions: Choose a character from your book whom you would like to get to know as a friend. We learn about people by what they say, how they act, and what others tell us. We learn about characters in books this way, too. As you read, write down information about the character you chose. Be sure to include page numbers and specific details.

What does the character look like?	**How does the character act with friends and family?**
1. _____	1. _____
2. _____	2. _____
3. _____	3. _____

Name of Character

_____

What problems does the character face?	**How does the character solve his/her problems?**
1. _____	1. _____
2. _____	2. _____
3. _____	3. _____

Why do you like this character? Write your answer on the back.

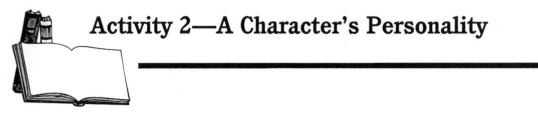

Activity 2—A Character's Personality

Purpose of the Activity

The purpose of this activity is for students to look for specific information, to draw inferences, and to understand the main character's personality, support a choice, and apply the concept of personality traits. The students will practice moving beyond the text as they read. After completion of the reading, they will gain greater understanding of people and themselves.

How to Use the Activity

Before this activity is used with a book, the students could practice it on themselves and substitute their own name for "character." It would be helpful to either list some personality traits on the board or to have the class brainstorm some personality traits and list them for all to view so students can possibly learn new vocabulary words as well. After this exercise, the students will feel more comfortable with the activity when discussing the many personality traits that make up a character in a book. To apply this concept to literature, this activity should be modeled with the class either during or after completion of the reading. When students are asked to make a decision on whether a particular trait is liked or not liked, they must support their answer. This critical thinking helps students make good judgments in decision making. By applying the trait to someone they know, students are making connections to the real world. The depth of understanding will depend on the age level of the students.

Evaluation

Assess this activity in terms of how well the students understand the main character and his/her personality by using specific examples from the book, how well they can support their choices, and how well they can relate a trait to a real person.

Variations

This activity can be expanded to a matching game after several books have been read. Students could be asked to match a picture of a character or the character's name to a group of possible personality traits. Students could be asked to draw concrete examples of traits for vocabulary reinforcement. For example, "kindness" could be represented with a drawing of someone picking up an item that someone else dropped.

Activity 2—A Character's Personality

Name: _____ Date: _____

Title: _____

Author: _____

Publisher and year: _____

Directions: Choose a character from your book who you like because of a trait in his/her personality. OR Choose a character from your book who you do not like because of a trait in his/her personality.

Character	**Trait**	**Like or Do Not Like**
_____	_____	_____

Tell 3 examples from the book when the character showed this trait.

1. _____

2. _____

3. _____

Tell 3 reasons why your like or do not like this trait in people.

1. _____

2. _____

3. _____

Write the name of someone you know who has this same trait. _____

Do you have this personality trait? _____

Write one trait that you have in your personality and explain how you know that this trait describes you?

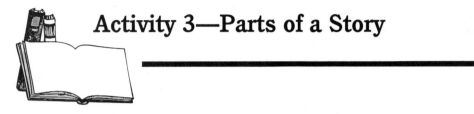

Activity 3—Parts of a Story

Purpose of the Activity

This reading and writing activity is designed to help students understand the important parts of a story as well as the whole book that they are reading. The activity can be used during or after reading. The goal is for students to look for these elements of fiction when they are reading independently.

How to Use the Activity

This activity should be used in three phases. The first phase consists of teaching through direct instruction, modeling by showing students how to complete the task, and controlling the discussion of the terms and responses. Using a simple traditional story would be ideal to help students become familiar with the form and terms. The first column can be used for definitions of the terms.

The second phase should consist of group discussion, and the second column on the sheet can be used for these responses. The third column of the form can be used for class responses that differ from the group's responses. Students sometimes find it difficult to understand that there is more than one acceptable response or correct interpretation to literature, so it is helpful to hear and write down other students' comments.

Finally, if you feel that the students understand the concepts, the third phase consists of having students work individually when filling out the second column. Once again, the third column can be used for comments from the class discussion. This last step creates student independence in learning.

Evaluation

The amount of credit given depends on which phase of instruction is being emphasized. Students working independently can receive a book project grade for their book. Give credit for note taking, participating in the activity, and discussing during phases one and two.

Variations

A variation of this activity is to change the third column to another story and work on comparing and contrasting two stories.

Activity 3—Parts of a Story

Elements Found in Every Story	Individual or Group Discussion	Class Discussion Responses
Title Author		
Plot—Events of story in one great sentence		
Problem in the story		
Main characters 1. 2. 3.		
Where and when—the story takes place		
Feeling of reader		
Clues of what might happen		
Who tells the story?		
What is the lesson in the story?		
Like or dislike the story and why?		

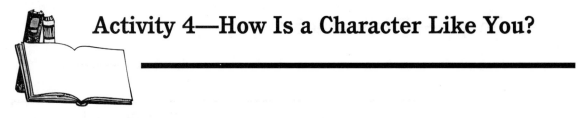

Activity 4—How Is a Character Like You?

Purpose of Activity

The purpose of this reading and writing activity is for students to become familiar with personality traits and descriptive language. This activity will also help students become careful readers while looking for events in the plot or behaviors of characters to support their choice of character trait. Students will increase vocabulary by using the words in the activity and through a preliminary discussion of the words.

How to Use the Activity

This activity can be assigned during or after reading. Discuss the vocabulary at the onset of the activity. Each trait can be assigned to a student and presented in the form of a vocabulary map. Students should list the part of speech, a synonym, an original sentence, and a picture of a face to help the understanding of the word. Students then need to list specific details from the novel to illustrate the chosen trait. They must decide whether they possess the trait themselves and then discuss their decisions in class.

Evaluation

The students should be evaluated on whether they followed directions and how much insight they gained through the activity. Ask students to write sentences using the new vocabulary words.

Variations

Have the students generate a list of character traits to choose from in the class, or have the children look for real people whom they know that possess similar traits and discuss the advantages and disadvantages of having that particular trait.

Activity 4—How Is a Character Like You?

Name: _____ Date: _____

Title: _____

Author: _____

Publisher and year: _____

Directions:
1. **Choose** an important character.
2. As you read your book, **look** for **descriptive adjectives** that describe the character. Adjectives are usually found before nouns and explain **how much, what kind,** and **how many.**
3. **Write** down the event or behavior that displays the trait listed. **Explain** if this trait is similar or different from you.

Character's Name _____

Trait/Adjective	Event or Behavior from the Story	Similar to or Different from Self

Some traits to consider: kind, trustworthy, friendly, honest, hardworking, serious, curious, interested, humorous, lazy, loud, talkative, helpful, questioning, sincere, cooperative

Activity 5—Class Newspaper

Purpose of the Activity

There are several purposes for this activity. The first is for students to use their reading and writing skills to create a project that shows inferential understanding of a book. Because readers must move beyond the literal text, they will practice their higher-level comprehension skills when writing a section of a newspaper. Students will learn different kinds and purposes of writing and the parts of a newspaper. Also, students must cooperate with a partner and a group in order to complete the entire newspaper.

How to Use the Activity

Use this activity as it is or add/delete newspaper sections depending on what parts of the newspaper the students are familiar with or what sections have been taught in class. This activity should be used after all students have finished reading the book. Depending on the number of students in the class and their ability, you may want to assign the parts, have the students choose their parts, or have the students randomly choose parts from a hat. If the class is large, then students can work in pairs, or more than one newspaper can be completed on the same book. After the newspaper is completed, the students can share their conclusions.

Evaluation

An individual project can be evaluated in terms of the standards set by the teacher (which are set forth when the assignment is given). Consider accuracy, creativity, originality, neatness, format, ability to meet a deadline, and completion of the part assigned. Before the newspaper is put together on construction paper, butcher block paper, or poster board, each individual or pair can present the assigned part to the class. During the sharing session, each person can be given a grade for sharing or a zero for not sharing. The entire newspaper can be given a grade upon completion.

Variations

If more than one book is read in a class, the members of the group that read a particular book can work together to create a newspaper about their book. Each group can then present their whole project to other groups. Also, students can look for blank space inside an actual newspaper to place their writing or project to make it look more authentic. Students can also create a mini-magazine instead of a newspaper. For young children, the newspapers can be pictorial and focus on the importance of the five "Ws" of news: who, what, when, where, why.

Activity 5—Class Newspaper

Name: _____ Date: _____

Title: _____

Author: _____

Publisher and year: _____

Directions: You are going to create a class newspaper about the book. Each group will be responsible for a particular part to help complete the class project.

Here are some suggestions:

1. **Editing**—Proofread the sections and put all the parts together.

2. **News article**—Write an article about an important event from the book that contains Who, What, When, Where, and Why.

3. **Editorial**—Write an essay discussing an issue from the book. State an opinion and support it with facts from the book.

4. **Feature article**—Write an article that states the message of the book and apply it to the world.

5. **Book review**—Write a review that discusses the positive and negative points as well as suggests who should read the book.

6. **Interview a character**—Pretend that you can interview a character and write several questions with the answers from the character's mind.

7. **Advertisement**—Create a one-page ad promoting the book to get others to read it.

8. **Crossword puzzle**—Create a puzzle and an answer key for important vocabulary words.

9. **Comics**—Create a comic strip with a key idea from the book.

10. **"Dear Abby" letter and response**—Write a letter about a problem in the book and then help solve the problem.

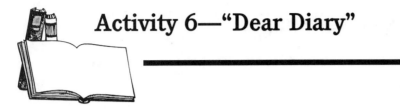

Activity 6—"Dear Diary"

Purpose of the Activity

This activity concentrates on higher-level reading and on diary writing. Because a diary is a vehicle for response writing, students will learn about putting feelings, reactions, and insights on paper and will have an opportunity to do so from a fictitious point of view. A lesson in point of view might be necessary to help students understand that response writing can vary greatly depending on the person doing the reacting. Finally, students will practice using facts and details from the book to explain the character's reactions in the diary entries.

How to Use the Activity

As a pre-reading/pre-writing exercise, you may want to find out who has prior knowledge about diary writing and discuss the purposes of writing to oneself. The concept could be modeled in class through journal writing. Students can be given time in class to read and record notes for their diary entries. If the class is more independent, students can read their books on their own, and this activity can be used as a post-reading activity. This activity could be used as a choice of several projects offered to students reading the same book or a variety of reading materials.

Evaluation

Because this activity is basically a writing assignment, the teacher can stress that all entries be mechanically correct. This activity can be graded as other writing assignments would be graded. If the element of creativity is required, a portion of the evaluation can be for creativity and originality.

Variations

One possibility for creativity and variety is to allow students to personalize the diary in terms of the characters in the book. The choice of paper (color and size), ink, illustrations, and informality of language can all be suggested or required at your discretion. The more choices the students have, the more opportunities they have to display their creativity and understanding of a character.

Activity 6—"Dear Diary"

Name: _____ Date:_____

Title: _____

Author: _____

Publisher and year: _____

Directions: Pretend you are one of the characters in your book. As you read, keep a diary. Each entry should be at least a paragraph in length.

Date _____

Dear Diary,

Today I _____

_____

_____

_____

_____

I feel like _____

_____

_____

_____

_____

Yours,

_____

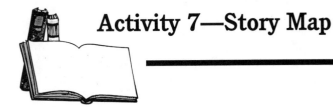

Activity 7—Story Map

Purpose of the Activity

The purpose of this writing activity is for students to show their understanding of a book by writing down their ideas. Because all stories contain the same basic elements of fiction, using the elements of fiction repeatedly in a graphic organizer helps the students see the similarities among all stories. The story map provides students with a way of keeping track of important information from the story as they read, as they are read to by the teacher, or during discussion after they have finished the book.

How to Use the Activity

Define the terms and model the use of the story map before students complete the form on their own. A simple, traditional story can be used before the activity is used with a book. If older students are familiar with the terms, they can work individually, in pairs, or in groups. This activity is also helpful for class discussions.

Evaluation

You may choose to evaluate this activity as a class assignment or as homework. The amount of credit for this activity will depend on its purpose. The items to consider are completeness, accuracy, and compliance with your guidelines.

Variations

You can make changes to the form if more or less information is desired. Another suggestion is for students to practice summary writing. On the back of the activity sheet, you can have the students write either a one-sentence or one-paragraph summary of the book. Summary writing is sometimes difficult for students because they need to include the beginning, middle, and end of a story in a particular format. This activity can be made into a template on the computer so that students can fill it in and gain word processing practice.

Activity 7—Story Map

Name: _____ Date:_____

Title: _____

Author: _____

Publisher and year: _____

Setting

Where: _____   When: _____

Main Characters
Most Important Character: _____

Two Descriptive Words: _____ , _____

Another Character: _____

Two Descriptive Words: _____ , _____

Problem in the Story _____

Events or Happenings in the Story

Beginning: _____

Middle: _____

End: _____

Feeling of the Reader _____

Something to Remember _____

Opinion of the Book _____

_____

_____

Activity 8—Letter to a Friend

Purpose of the Activity

The purpose of this activity is to provide a vehicle for students to communicate to other students about a book that they are reading or have just read. The inclusion of questions within the framework of the letter allows students to answer the letter if you want them to pursue the communication further. In addition, the students learn the format of a friendly letter.

How to Use the Activity

Depending on the ability of the students, you can use this form as a frame for students to follow specifically, or you may want to use it as an example for students, loosely adding, changing, or deleting the requested information. Letter writing between students can be done in a class or outside of class. The writing can be done in the classroom or in a computer lab, where students can change seats and read each other's letter on the computer. Students will become more familiar with other books through the letter exchange.

Evaluation

This writing activity can be used as a post-reading book report, or it can be used as a writing assignment while students are reading. Communication among students can take place while they read their books so that more questions can be asked. Readers would be able to answer the questions as more of the book is read. Grade the writing in terms of the accurate content, compliance with letter format, and/or writing skills.

Variations

After students become familiar with letter writing, you can brainstorm other topics and questions to be included in a letter about the book. This activity is particularly interesting if students in the class read a variety of books. This project can be used in conjunction with teaching the business letter. A comparison and contrast discussion can help students understand the format differences of the two types of writing and purposes for each type of letter.

Activity 8—Letter to a Friend

Name: _____

Title: _____

Author: _____

Publisher and year: _____

Directions: Write a letter to a friend in the class about your book. You can use this form as a rough draft to include important information about the book.

Date _____

Dear _____ ,

    I am reading (*or I have just finished reading*) a book called _____ _____ by _____ , the author. It was about a character named _____ who has a problem. The problem is _____ . The story is about_____ _____ .

    I like/dislike (*circle one*) this book because _____ _____ .

    This would be a really great book for someone to read if they like _____ _____ . The next book that I would like to read would be a _____ . Write back soon about the book that you are reading (*or have just finished*). Let me know about these things in your book:_____ , _____ , _____ . (*Name three things or ask three questions that you would like to know about your friend's book.*) Talk to you soon. Bye.

Sincerely,

(*Sign your name here*)

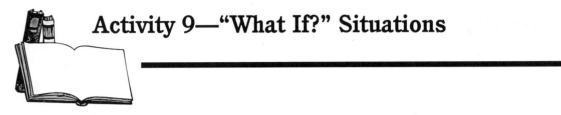

Activity 9—"What If?" Situations

Purpose of the Activity

The purpose of this reading/writing activity is to have students write creatively using their imaginations and inferences about a characters' personality and then support their choices. Students must make educated guesses based on their understanding of a character. Although there is no single correct response to any of the questions, the students must provide specific details to justify their responses.

How to Use the Activity

This activity can be used as a writing assignment in class, for homework, or as a test. The students can share their writing with other members of the class as a springboard for discussion and debate.

Evaluation

This activity can be graded as any other writing assignment would be graded. You can determine how many sentences, details, or paragraphs are required. Rather than you grading the piece of writing alone, students can be involved in the process by looking for details that prove their classmates' contentions.

Variations

Students often enjoy the creativity of this unusual essay format. An interesting variation is to ask the students to write "What if?" questions and after screening the choices, have students choose questions from a hat. A prewriting activity could also be used by asking students first to answer "What if?" questions with themselves as the first-person point of view. Some suggestions could be:

What if you won a million dollars? How would you spend the money?

What if you were king or queen for a day? What would you do?

What if you could have three wishes? What would they be and why?

What if you could only save three items in a disaster? What would they be and why?

What if you could go anywhere in the world? Where would you go and why?

Activity 9—"What If?" Situations

Name: _____ Date: _____

Title: _____

Author: _____

Publisher and year: _____

Directions: Choose one of the situations for a character that you liked from one of the books you read. Write a few sentences with three reasons that explain your answer.

1. What if you could choose a character to be a friend (or a pet)? Who would you choose and why?

2. What if you could be a character in one the stories you have read? Which story would you choose and why?

3. What if you could choose a gift for a main character? What would that gift be and why?

4. What if you could write your own story about a character about whom you have read? What would your story be about?

5. What if you and a character could go out for a day of fun? What would the two of you do and why?

Name of Character

_____

Write some ideas here and on the back:

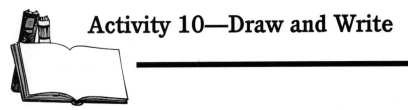

Activity 10—Draw and Write

Purpose of the Activity

The purpose of this reading/writing activity is for students to practice visualizing both during and after their reading. Students need to recreate a scene from memory by using all five senses to help the words in print be more meaningful for them as readers. This activity involves students reading carefully for details and looking back in the book for descriptions or actions as necessary. The students get the opportunity to be illustrators as well as writers.

How to Use the Activity

In order for this activity to be valuable, some preliminary work may need to be done. You may want to give a mini lesson on sensory imagery both in pictures and in print. Modeling examples from the real world will help clarify the concept. You may want to discuss the role of an illustrator and the role of a writer. These two people may not necessarily work together, yet both are communicating ideas. Sometimes the same person works in both capacities. Students need not feel they have to duplicate the original work. Try to discourage copying.

Evaluation

Give credit to students who complete the assignment and give logical reasons for their choices. Encourage open discussion and be willing to accept diversity. You may even want to have students label their senses and give credit for sharing with the class.

Variations

This activity could be expanded into a review for several books that were read by a class. If all class members were to complete this activity, students could be asked to guess which scene matched which book. Place the books on the blackboard ledge, and place the students' scenes on the blackboard with magnets. Students can take turns matching the pictures with the books.

For older children, students can draw symbols or find symbols in clipart for their favorite characters. The same game can be played as above except that the students will be matching the symbols of characters with the books.

Activity 10—Draw and Write

Name: _____ Date: _____

Title: _____

Author: _____

Publisher and year: _____

Directions:
1. Think of an important part or your favorite part in the book that you have read.
2. Try to visualize (picture in your head) the scene with all the details. The details could be sights, colors, sounds, tastes, smells, and feelings that you remember.
3. Try to draw this scene and tell why it is important to the story or why it is your favorite.

Draw here:

Write here:

_____

_____

_____

Activity 11—Writing a Newspaper Article

Purpose of the Activity

There are several purposes for this reading/writing activity as the students are asked to use their reading, judging, writing, and critical thinking skills to accomplish this task. First, the students will read a book and complete an activity picking out important, detailed information. Second, the students will improve their reading because they will learn to read for a specific purpose and relate fictional material to real-world possibilities. Third, the students will draft and write a nonfiction, informational newspaper article in a particular format to learn about journalistic writing. Last, the students will display their understanding of the information and the book by drawing a picture and writing a caption for the story.

How to Use the Activity

This activity can be assigned during reading so that the students can read carefully and document meaningful events from the book that would make good front-page stories. If you assign this activity after the students have finished reading the book, they can go back to the book and make judgments about the incidents in order to choose one to write about in the news story. To increase background knowledge, review the form of a news story and have the students read samples themselves or read sample news stories to them. For the younger children, you might consider pairing or grouping students after a book or story has been read to them. At all levels, modeling the activity is very important for increased success.

Evaluation

The students' projects should be evaluated in terms of whether the project followed the assignment's directions. Another consideration is the quality of the newspaper story and its accuracy in following details from the book. A third consideration is the creativity of the layout and picture, the headlines, and possibly the sharing of the story with the class. Students can be involved in evaluating the project by looking for accuracy, deciding which are the best news stories, and explaining the reasons for their choices.

Variations

Students can look in a newspaper for blank spaces to cut out and save so that the typed articles can be pasted onto them and made to look like a real newspaper. Depending on how much of the newspaper and its parts you want to teach, you can also ask part of the class to write a feature story based on a human-interest topic discussed in the book. Then you and the class can discuss the news and feature stories and why their placement in the newspaper is so important.

Activity 11—Writing a Newspaper Article

Name: _____

Title: _____

Author: _____

Publisher and year: _____

Directions:

1. Select an important event from your book and write a news story that would make the front page of the newspaper if the event were true. All news stories include the five Ws (who, what, where, when, why) plus how. Use this outline to plan your article. Then write your story on separate paper.

    Who _____   **What** _____

    When _____   **Where** _____

    Why _____   **How** _____

2. Think of a catchy headline to use as a title for the news story.

    _____

3. Draw an illustration and write a caption to be included with the story.

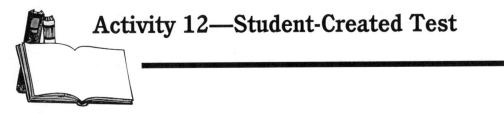

Activity 12—Student-Created Test

Purpose of the Activity

There are several purposes for this reading/writing activity. First, the students must follow a format and specific directions on how to write a test about their book. Second, they get the experience of writing a test. Third, they will focus on the main points and details that they feel are important enough to be tested on. Last, the students must take the test to provide an answer key that will demonstrate their knowledge about the book.

How to Use the Activity

This activity can be used immediately after reading a book or as an alternative to a book report. The class can read a single book, or individuals can choose their own books. You can choose questions from the students' tests to make up a test for the class. Students can also take each other's tests, if the quality of the tests meets your standards.

Evaluation

The students' test projects can be graded as any book report would be. Some factors to consider are the ability of the students to follow the directions of the format, the focus of the questions on content, and the accuracy of the answer key in terms of facts, details, and inferences made from the novel.

Variations

Change the format of the test or even eliminate it by asking the students to brainstorm the different kinds of tests that they like and find effective. Of course, you can add to or subtract from the information asked for in the activity.

In my experience, students tend to write much more difficult tests than teachers do, so a mini lesson on important story parts such as plot, setting, mood, characters, and theme, and/or how to ask good questions could be incorporated. The level of the students will determine how involved you want the task to be.

Activity 12—Student-Created Test

Name: _____ Date: _____

Title: _____

Author: _____

Publisher and year: _____

Directions: Your group is to create a test on the book you have read. Then you will exchange tests with another group and take the test.

Part 1. Write **2 multiple choice questions** about the major events of the story.

Part 2. Write **3 questions that can be matched with choices**. These questions should be about the characters.

Part 3. Write **3 fill in the blank questions**. These should be short-answer blanks about the setting.

Part 4. Write **2 true or false sentences** about the message of the book.

This makes a **total of 10 questions**.

Make sure you have an answer sheet separate from the test.

The teacher must receive the answer key along with the test.

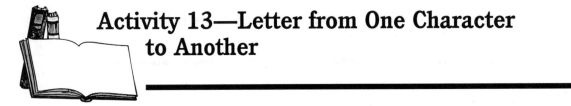

Activity 13—Letter from One Character to Another

Purpose of the Activity

Although this is primarily a writing activity, the students must have read part or all of a book to understand the characters enough to think and write as the characters would. Also, depending on the choice of topics, the students will discuss their understanding of the major issue of the story or the elements of the story. Finally, the students will learn the parts of a friendly letter and practice this form of communication.

How to Use the Activity

This activity can be used during or after reading. The students will probably have the greatest understanding of the characters at the conclusion of the reading. However, if you want the students to make predictions, discuss a problem, or help in the decision process, then this activity would be useful during the reading of the book. It might be useful for students to share their letters with a partner or the entire class. This would allow them to discuss each other's feelings as well as to critique and question what others think and have written. For younger students in particular, more prewriting time may be needed on the topic of characterization. One possibility would be to ask the class to write about a topic from the book and share the responses. Point out that different opinions and ideas form because of personalities and experiences.

Evaluation

The students' written project should be evaluated as any piece of writing would be assessed, or students can discuss the topic in the letter and the writer's accuracy and insight into the character. The assessment can be done in the form of a simple rubric, with the expectations made clear to all students. The class can vote for the best letters and then assess them.

Variations

In addition to writing to a character in the book, the letters can be randomly passed out to students so they can be answered as an in-class writing assignment. Return the letters for the students to read the responses. Students like to correspond with one another, and this activity would allow them to do so as they take on the personalities and points of view of the characters from the book.

Activity 13—Letter from One Character to Another

Name: _____ Date: _____

Title: _____

Author: _____

Publisher and year: _____

Directions: Pretend you are one of the characters from your book. Write a friendly letter to another character in the book discussing one of the topics below.

1. Describe a problem and ask for suggestions on handling it. Make sure to stay in character and write what the character would write.

    or

2. Explain an event from the book that changed your character's life.

_____   _____

Date

Dear (*Name of Character*),

     (*Make it clear which of the above topics you are writing about by giving a short explanation of the plot.*)

     (*You may want to ask questions that you want the person to whom you are writing to answer.*)

Sincerely,

(*Sign your name here*)

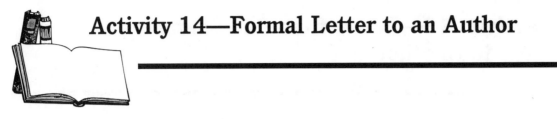

Activity 14—Formal Letter to an Author

Purpose of the Activity

There are several purposes for this writing/reading activity. First, the students must read a book carefully and critically, with the purpose of corresponding with the writer and offering their opinions of the work. Second, the students must learn the business letter format in order to complete the writing assignment. Third, the students are writing to a real person, who hopefully will answer their letters and involve them in real-life communication. Fourth, the students can research information about the author and his or her background so they can ask intelligent questions.

How to Use the Activity

This activity can be used when students read a variety of books in class or when students read a book of their own choosing. Each student can write to a different person so that the class learns about a variety of authors. When the students start reading, tell them that they will be writing to the authors of their books, so they should take notes on likes and dislikes as they read. The notes will provide students with specific information to include in the letter. You can provide the students with addresses for the authors or you can have the students do this research themselves. For younger students, one possibility is for students to write to authors in care of the publishers of their books. Use the form for this activity as a guide or rough draft for students to give them ideas and show them the business letter format.

Evaluation

This activity should consist of an initial rough draft of the letter, a final draft to be graded, and a corrected perfect copy to be sent to the author. A grade can also be given for addressing an envelope correctly and enclosing the folded letter properly.

Variations

Students can use the school's address or their home address on the envelope for replies. If home addresses are used, the students can bring in the replies to share with the class for extra credit. Make a copy of the replies for a file for future reference.

Activity 14—Formal Letter to an Author

Name: _____ Date: _____

Title: _____

Author: _____

Publisher and year: _____

Directions: Use the form below as a rough draft.

_____

Your address _____
Your city, state, zip code _____

Date _____

Name of author _____
Address of author _____
City, state, zip code of author _____

Dear Mr. or Ms. _____:

My name is _____ and I go to _____
school. I just finished reading (*name of book underlined*) _____
_____ . I liked it because
(*Tell what you liked about the book, a character, or the book's topic and why*)

_____

_____ .

My favorite part was _____

_____ .

I was wondering (*ask a question*) _____

_____ .

Sincerely,
(*Write your name*)

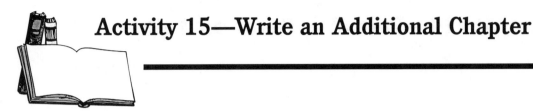

Activity 15—Write an Additional Chapter

Purpose of the Activity

The main purpose of this writing activity is for students to think, make predictions, and write creatively by adding a chapter to the book they have just finished reading. The students must make inferences about the characters' future and behavior that are consistent with what the characters have said and done in the book already.

How to Use the Activity

Assign one or all of the choices listed for additional chapters. You can brainstorm with the class on one of the choices and have the students discuss the positive and negative points of having the book continue in such a manner. A full-page brainstorming sheet is included on page 32. The students can also work in groups as they pre-write, outline/plan, draft, revise, edit, and proofread. This project can easily include mini lessons on the writing process and/or mechanics. Another suggestion is to allow students to share their writing with other individuals, groups, or the entire class. Reading an individual's or group's work to an audience helps instill pride and promote oral fluency.

Evaluation

Evaluate the additional chapter to the book as a writing assignment and grade it according to the conditions set forth for the class. Some factors to consider are the writing process, group cooperation, length requirements, and content. Each chapter's content could be discussed and voted on by the class members, noting such elements as accuracy, characterization, plot continuity, and resolution of the story. Sharing writing with class members could also be part of the entire grade.

Variations

A variation for this activity might be one of the following: ask students to add a new character to the story, change the setting of the story, remove an action of the plot, or change the personality of a character. By doing any of these rewrites, students learn that both plot and theme can be affected.

Activity 15—Write an Additional Chapter

Name: _____ Date:_____

Title: _____

Author: _____

Publisher and year: _____

Directions: After you finish your book, write an additional chapter that could be added on at the end of the story. You must make predictions based on the information that you already know from reading the book. Below are some suggestions.

1. Write about what happens to the main character either immediately after the end of the story or five years in the future.

2. Write about the next day or the next week of a character's life.

3. Many times an author ends a story and you still have questions about what may have happened. Here is your chance to complete the story.

You may want to think of ideas before you write here:

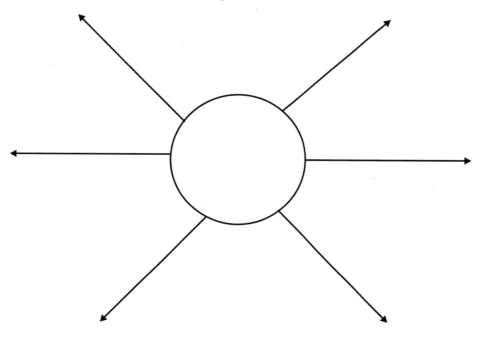

Brainstorming Sheet
Use this form to organize your ideas.

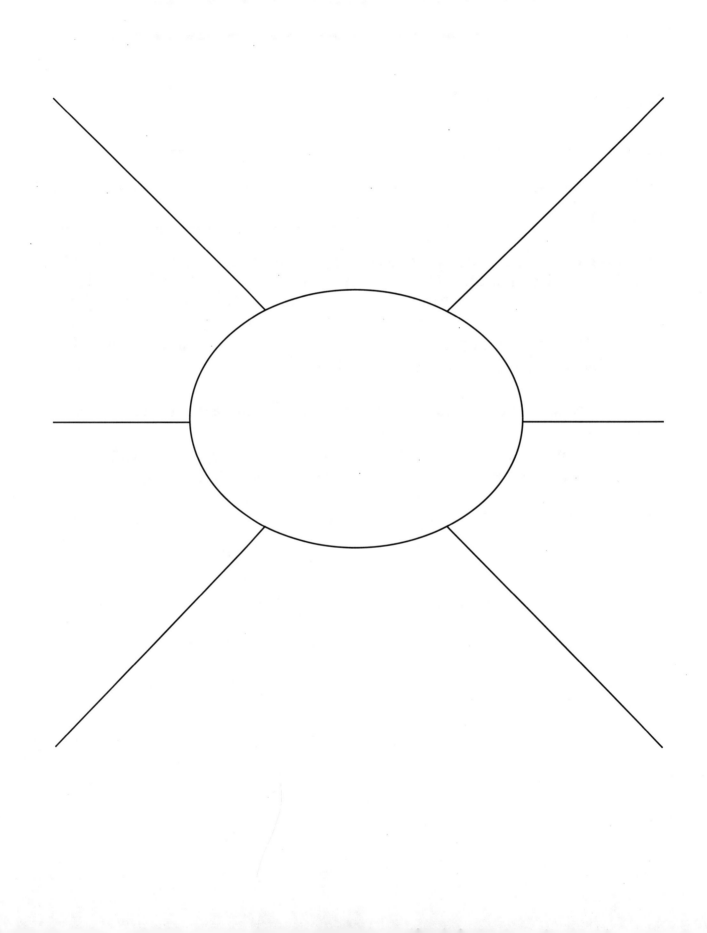

Activity 16—Write a New Ending

Purpose of the Activity

This post-reading activity has two purposes. First, this activity involves inference skills and application skills. Students must understand the characters and the plot in order to replace the author's ending. The plot sequence must make sense and be logical according to the preceding action. Second, the students practice their creative writing skills by actually being authors. Because they must justify their reasons for changing the ending, they are learning to support choices with reasons and facts.

How to Use the Activity

This activity should be assigned after the students have finished reading the book. The suggestions on the activity sheet are to help point the students toward directions to pursue in writing. You can assign particular suggestions to individuals or groups if the entire class is reading the same book. Another possibility is to allow students to choose the directions that they wish the new ending to follow. Pairing students to listen to each other's rough drafts will enable peer editors to check for whether the new ending makes sense, is logical, and accurately uses facts and details from the book.

Evaluation

The students' assessment can include the writing process as well as the final product. The writing process should include the steps of pre-writing, drafting, editing, and revising until a final draft is turned in as a new chapter. You might have the new endings read aloud to the whole class, and the class can choose the best new ending. This would give the students practice in their reading, listening, and speaking skills.

Variations

One variation for this activity is for students to think beyond the idea of a new ending and create a new character who can be introduced during the book or at the new ending. Students can write a new story that features new characters. For smaller children, an illustration of the new character would make the person or animal more real. Also, the new endings could be illustrated as a page in a book. You could explain the author and illustrator roles and how the visualization must communicate what is in print.

Another possibility is to have the students create an ending that would allow the author to write a sequel. The students can also write a first chapter for a new book and begin the plot where the original book ends. The students can also imagine what the story would have been like if the setting had been changed or a character had been eliminated. Ask the students to suggest story variations.

Activity 16—Write a New Ending

Name: _____ Date:_____

Title: _____

Author: _____

Publisher and year: _____

Directions: Did you like the ending of the book? Can you think of another way to end the story? Write a new ending.

Here are some suggestions:

1.   Change the way the problem in the story is solved.

2.   Have the main character learn or not learn something.

3.   Have the ending changed from a happy ending to a sad ending or the other way around.

4.   Add new information about the characters so you can reveal a new ending.

5.   Add new evidence or facts that can be found in the story to help solve a mystery or suspense story in a different way.

6.   Add a new character to the story who would affect the other characters and the ending.

Come up with ideas of your own. Be creative and brainstorm ideas here!

Activity 17—Choosing a Character As a Friend

Purpose of the Activity

There are several purposes for this during- and after-reading activity. First, the activity involves the students in expository writing that gives them practice in supporting one's opinions with facts and details from a text. It also teaches the students paragraph format and the use of transitions in writing. Finally, the students make critical judgments, which are necessary in life, especially when choosing friends. The values that the students find important will become apparent by the character they choose to have as a friend, which will open up discussion in the classroom.

How to Use the Activity

While the students are reading their novel, tell them the topic of the writing assignment so they can take notes and look and listen for information while they read or are being read to in the classroom. Another approach to the activity is for students to be given the topic as a post-reading activity in which they must go back into the book to look for support for their contentions. With this approach, the students must do more analysis afterward and become familiar enough with the text to locate specific information. You can choose which approach is better for your students based on their abilities and your goals.

Evaluation

The writing project can be graded like any other writing assignment. Some factors to consider are content, writing skills, and ability to follow directions. The students' ability to meet a deadline is another consideration.

Variations

A variation for this writing assignment is to assign the topic for a theme of several paragraphs in length, depending on the grade level. The assignment can also be given as one of several writing topics from which students can make their selections. Give students the choice to write about who they would *not* want to have as a friend. Also, the students can share their writing assignments with other members of the class and discuss their choices. The activity form can be used as a rough or final draft.

Activity 17—Choosing a Character As a Friend

Name: _____ Date: _____

Title: _____

Author: _____

Publisher and year: _____

Directions: Write a paragraph of at least _____ sentences in which you explain the reasons for choosing a particular character from your novel whom you would like to have as a friend. Give specific information from the book for your support. Use the pattern below to help you with the writing.

Name of character _____

Title of Paper

(*Topic sentence*) It would be exciting or fun or special or _____ (*choose one descriptive word*) to be a friend of _____ from the novel _____ by _____ for many reasons.

First, _____
_____.

Second, _____
_____.

Third, _____
_____.

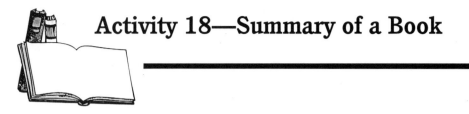

Activity 18—Summary of a Book

Purpose of the Activity

There are several purposes for this post-reading activity. First, the activity requires higher-level thinking and evaluating skills as well as some creativity in order to complete the task. The students are asked to rate the book using stars to show their opinion of the novel's worth. Second, they must use their creativity to draw a symbol to represent the book. Third, they need to condense many ideas into a small number of words in order to write a summary.

How to Use the Activity

Students can use the following page as a prepared form or they can use a computer or paper and markers to design a symbol to represent the book. Then they should write, type, or cut and paste the information to fit into the object. The symbol should be large enough to contain several sentences of information, depending on the discretion of the teacher and the age group. By having the students write inside this limited space, it forces them to carefully choose their words for specific meaning. You may want to model the process of summary writing first. Students need to remember that good summaries contain a beginning, middle, and end. You may want the students to share their projects with other students.

Evaluation

This book project can be evaluated as any written assignment would be assessed. Besides the accuracy of the information, consider whether the students met the requirements of the assignment by completing the written information on the activity sheet. The creative element is always difficult to assess, but as long as the students have good reasons for choosing symbols that they consider appropriate for their books, the objects are acceptable.

Variations

The students can display their objects on a bulletin board or in some other fashion. If the class is reading a variety of books, have the students match an object and its information with the correct book. Finally, the quotes can be used as reader responses at a later time.

Activity 18—Summary of a Book

Name: _____ Date: _____

Title: _____

Author: _____

Publisher and year: _____

Rating (one to five stars with five being the highest) _____

Directions: Think of a symbol that can represent the entire book in some way. Draw it large enough to include the following information.

- ◆ Three- to five-sentence summary of the story
- ◆ A phrase or sentence worth quoting
- ◆ One sentence stating what you liked or disliked about the story

Activity 19—Vocabulary Exchange

Purpose of the Activity

The purpose of this activity involves vocabulary and contextual meanings of words. First, the readers must consider the type of word to choose and, for older students, its part of speech, in order to successfully replace the word with two others of the same type and meaning. Next, the students' peers share and evaluate each other's choices. Finally, students practice working with the thesaurus and dictionary and learn how important word choices are for a writer.

How to Use the Activity

Use this activity with a book during or after reading. You can choose the page and/or passage or allow the students to choose their own. This activity can be assigned in addition to another book project. Students may or may not be allowed to use dictionaries or thesauruses, depending on the vocabulary of class members. You can use a passage from a book as a model for a class discussion so students understand how to proceed on their own. You can also have students work in pairs or groups to discuss word choices.

Evaluation

This activity can be assessed as a class activity or as a homework assignment. Remember that changing a particular word can sometimes change the meaning of a sentence or passage. Students should become aware of this as they discuss each other's word choices.

Variations

If you wish to teach a little more grammar for older students, you can have the students label the part of speech of the words they underlined in the passage they chose for the task. The students could help each other understand how words are used in sentences. Students could be required to work on word choice in their own writing in journals or homework. You can extend this exercise even further by having students do some or all of the above on their own compositions in the future.

Activity 19—Vocabulary Exchange

Name: _____ Date:_____

Title: _____

Author: _____

Publisher and year: _____

Directions: Select part of a page from your book and find 5 words that you did not know or words that are new to you. Then find two synonyms that can replace each word.

Page number in novel: _____

NEW WORD	SYNONYM	SYNONYM
1.		
2.		
3.		
4.		
5.		

Now ask a classmate to read the passage with your synonyms. Does your classmate think the meaning changes with the change in vocabulary?

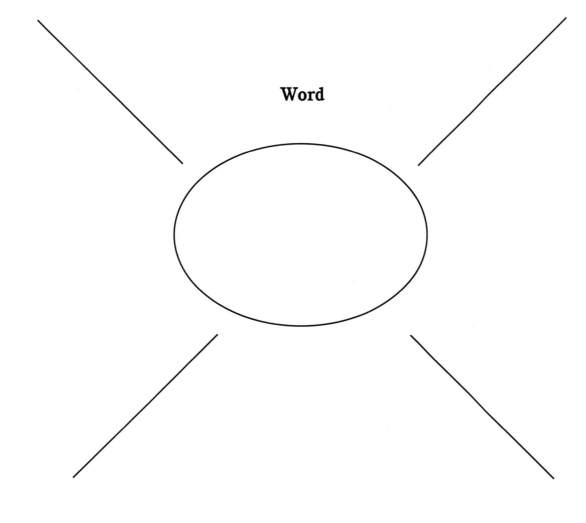

Definition

Synonym

Word

Your Own Sentence

Draw a Picture

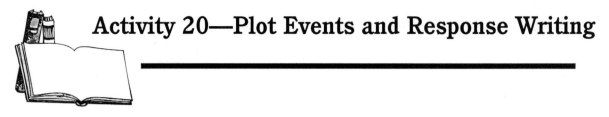

Activity 20—Plot Events and Response Writing

Purpose of the Activity

There are several purposes for this activity. The main one is to actively involve the students in the reading process. By having the students write a summary of what was just read, they must think about the material, understand the action, condense the ideas, and write a concise statement. The response writing involves the students by having them interact with the text and make connections in the form of a prediction, question, reaction, or opinion.

How to Use the Activity

This during-reading activity should be used by the students each time they read the book. For longer books, plan sustained silent reading for the first ten minutes of class to work on the reading and writing. For shorter books, you can pause at appropriate places if you are reading out loud to the class. The activity should be modeled at first so that the difference between summary and response is understood. All the entries can be collected at the end of the reading. You determine the number of entries that are required. Duplicate the form as needed.

Evaluation

Grade the participation of the students for making entries and on the accuracy of the events and personal connections. You can use this activity as a project in itself or as background preliminary information for a larger assignment, such as one for older students on all the elements of fiction.

Variations

Instead of logging ideas per chapter, have students log each time they read, whether the chapter is completed or not. An advantage to following this format is to have students accountable for every class and home reading if a certain number of entries are required. This form is useful for oral or silent readings. The more connections that students make while reading, the more meaning the text will have for them.

Activity 20—Plot Events and Response Writing

Name: _____ Date: _____

Title: _____

Author: _____

Publisher and year: _____

Directions: As you read your book, write a one-sentence plot summary and a response statement for each chapter on this form. Make sure to include the date for each entry.

Plot = actual events from the book

Response = a prediction, question, reaction, and/or opinion about what you liked, disliked, or found interesting

	Date	Summary and Response Sentences
1.		Plot Response
2.		Plot Response
3.		Plot Response

Date		Summary and Response Sentences
4.		Plot Response
5.		Plot Response
6.		Plot Response
7.		Plot Response
8.		Plot Response
9.		Plot Response
10.		Plot Response

Part II

Representing and Viewing
Standards Activities

Activity 21—Poster Advertisement

Purpose of the Activity

This representational activity/project is a post-reading one because the students must use higher-level thinking skills to draw inferences about the characters, symbols, and theme of the book. They must also write a short persuasive review. The main purpose of the representing/viewing project is for the students to design posters for their books that promote the reading of the book by others, in particular their classmates. The posters display the students' knowledge and understanding of the books. A book review is included as part of the activity so that the students can make solid judgments and learn to support their beliefs. Drawings and pictures allow for creativity and variation and teach students about the placement of graphics and information on a poster. This activity leads into presenting the poster to the class to discuss the book further.

How to Use the Activity

This activity can be assigned after a class book or individual books have been read. If the class has read a variety of books, oral presentations on the posters allow the students to become familiar with many titles for future reading. Depending on the ability of the class, you can have the students work in class or on their own. Give students flexibility to add or change requested information. The teacher should decide the size of the poster (two feet by two feet is large enough so that all class members can see it during the presentation). Butcher block paper, poster board, or art paper works well. Before the task, view movie posters, billboards, or other advertisements and have students write observations in a journal for a discussion about placement and other details of a catchy appearance.

Evaluation

The poster project can be graded on a variety of factors such as accuracy, attractiveness, completeness of information, insights, ability to meet a deadline, and creativity. Students should be given the criteria at the onset of the project. Sharing of the project can also be graded. Sometimes, to relieve students' anxiety, a simple "A" or "0" can be given for the experience of presenting orally. You can decide on the weight of the grade.

Variations

Ask students to brainstorm what information should be placed on a poster, and give the students more flexibility in the actual design of the project. This activity can be used as one of several choices for book projects.

Activity 21—Poster Advertisement

Name: _____ Date:_____

Title: _____

Author: _____

Publisher and year: _____

Directions: Create a poster to promote your book. Follow the example below. You should try to show creativity, originality, and an understanding of the book.

Write catchy phrases.
Examples: "I liked it! You will too!"
"Read this book!"

<u>Title</u>

Author
Publisher and Year

Draw or paste pictures about the topic.

Write a one-sentence main idea.

Tell why you liked a particular part and why you liked the whole book.

Tell why others should read it.

Activity 22—Collage

Purpose of the Activity

This activity not only involves reading and some writing, but it also emphasizes the standards of representing and viewing. The students are given the opportunity to represent the book's major ideas in the form of a collage, a careful placement of a variety of pictures and words which display an appropriate theme or motif from the book. This hands-on activity allows students to be creative and original with their ideas as well as think symbolically. This activity can be shared with others through a presentation and explanation of the pictorial representation. When students do formal booktalks on their books and collages, they share their knowledge and connections with the book with others. They also practice their speaking skills in front of an audience, and the class members learn how to act appropriately as an audience.

How to Use the Activity

This activity can be used after a book has been finished. If an entire class has read the same book, class members can sign up for different themes, motifs, or topics present in the work. For their collages, the choices listed on the worksheet are popular themes that apply to many books. You may alter them as needed. After the collages are completed, you may want students to share projects with one another as one-minute booktalks. The points listed on the activity sheet can help you to grade students for their talks.

Evaluation

For assessment, evaluate the quality of the collage and the accuracy of and explanation for the pictorial display. At the beginning of the reading, the students should know what the criteria are for the assessment. The presentation and the expectations for the audience should be discussed with the students. The presentation can be graded as a speech, or it can be counted as a sharing experience where students would receive a grade of credit or no credit.

Variations

The class members can brainstorm the themes or messages for the collages. Also, students can work in pairs or groups. Allow younger students to use class time to work on the project. Ask students to bring in old magazines, newspapers, and catalogs to cut up in the classroom. These can be saved for future projects.

Activity 22—Collage

Name: _____ Date:_____

Title: _____

Author: _____

Publisher and year: _____

Directions: Choose one of the themes (main ideas for a story) from below that seems appropriate for your book. Then look for or draw pictures, words, and symbols that display the theme. Be ready to explain your collage to your classmates. Circle your choice below and write one sentence about it.

_____

_____

Possible Choices:

1. Responsibility
2. Self discovery
3. Trust
4. Friendship
5. Value of time
6. Decisions
7. Love
8. Family
9. Losing something/someone
10. Honesty
11. Hard work
12. Pick one of your own

Presentation:

1. Tell the title, author, and publisher and show the book.
2. Show the collage to the class.
3. Explain why you chose the pictures that you did.
4. Say whether you liked the book and why or why not.

Suggestion:

The collage should be large enough for all members of the class to see.

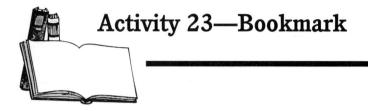

Activity 23—Bookmark

Purpose of Activity

There are several purposes for this reading, writing, representing, and viewing activity. The students must first read the novel and then write in a creative, concise manner. The bookmark format allows the students to be creative and original, but by giving them a specific format, you are requiring higher-level thinking skills and critical analysis in a defined space. Another purpose is for the students to use the bookmark in their next book. Students learn from one another by displaying the projects on a bulletin board in the classroom.

How to Use the Activity

This activity can be used as a post-reading project on a class book or individual books. You determine the size of the bookmark. The bookmark activity sheet or construction paper works well. Students can print, type, or use the computer to type the requested information about the book. For a greater learning experience, the students should share the information on their bookmarks with their peers either in groups or as a class presentation. Upon completion of the project, students often like the idea of laminating the bookmarks. Younger children may want to use paint, glitter, ribbons, or many colors for their decorations, which adds ownership to the bookmark and pride in reading the book.

Evaluation

The project can be evaluated by the specific criteria that you set up. Set up a rubric so all the bookmarks are evaluated in the same fashion. Consider content, cleverness, and completion of the assignment on time. The presentation can be counted as a separate grade.

Variations

All information for the bookmark can be altered to emphasize whatever points need to be stressed in teaching a particular book. One variation might be to ask for a quote from a peer who has also read the book. Children should look at sample bookmarks to get ideas for color, placement of graphics, and text. Publishers often create bookmarks for book promotion and marketing purposes. These can be obtained by contacting them.

Activity 23—Bookmark

Name: _____ Date: _____

Title: _____

Author: _____

Publisher and year: _____

Directions: Design a bookmark for your book. Follow the example and be original, clever, colorful, and creative. You can fold a piece of paper in half and begin planning. This could be a useful bookmark for your next book!

<u>Title</u>
Author's Name

A Catchy Phrase

A 3-Sentence Summary

Your Opinion of the Book

*Tell Why Others
Should Read It*

Your Name and the Date

Activity 24—Scrapbook for a Character

Purpose of the Activity

This project has several purposes. The first is for students to identify with a character from the book to view well-rounded characters as real people. For younger children, even though the main character may be an animal, there will still be human traits to identify with. Secondly, students must display their understanding of a character by making a scrapbook that the character would make based on the relationships of people in the book, decisions made in dealing with problems, and significant events that effected that character's life. The scrapbook can represent the students' insights, knowledge, and connections to a book through the eyes of a character and their interpretations of that character. The students can display their artistic and creative talents through their choices, design, and final product. Another goal is to have students share their projects with class members, so they can learn from each other.

How to Use the Activity

The project can be worked on individually, in pairs, or as a group. This project can also be assigned for a class reading the same book, with students signing up for minor characters and protagonists. Using several books allows for even more variety in a discussion of books and characters. Students should pre-write before beginning the project. Older students might even want to keep a log as they read to keep track of specific decisions, events, people, feelings, and objects they might want to refer to in the scrapbook. If possible, sample photographs or scrapbooks can be used as models in the classroom. Have the students make inferences based on the visual information. After students organize a plan or pattern for the project, they should draw, cut out, or find what they need for their scrapbooks. Having old magazines, newspapers, catalogs, and colored paper available in a supply box will help students get started and be successful. Students should label the selections within the scrapbook along with the significance of each entry. This helps the viewer understand the significance of each item in the scrapbook.

Evaluation

The scrapbook can be evaluated as a writing project, an artistic endeavor, and/or a sharing experience. The standards for the evaluation should be made clear to the students at the onset of the assignment. The oral sharing and viewing of the project can be done in front of the class with a set number of entries presented or shared in groups where the scrapbooks are passed around and talked about. The display of the projects in the room is often a celebration of a completed event.

Variations

This activity can be used as one of several projects for students to choose from. The power of choice gives those students who want to imagine themselves being a character a chance to do so, while others can choose an activity to match their learning style.

Activity 24—Scrapbook for a Character

Name: _____ Date:_____

Title: _____

Author: _____

Publisher and year: _____

Directions: Imagine that you are a character from the book. Make a scrapbook of pictures, objects, letters, and other items that you think the character would find important. You can include pictures of other characters, important events, or prized possessions. Bind the booklet in some way. Make sure that everything is labeled with how it is important to the character.

Name of character: _____

Name of the Item	Importance to the Character
1.	
2.	
3.	
4.	
5.	
6.	

Activity 25—Poster Story Map

Purpose of the Activity

This post-reading activity is a project that can involve all the standards of English and display students' understanding of a book or fiction story. The age and level of the students will determine the depth of the discussion of terminology. Because the students must also use pictures and drawings, they must be analytical and choose creative, colorful graphics that also have relationships to elements in the story. Another purpose for this activity is for the students to learn from one another as they share their analyses of the book with the class. As there may be more than one interpretation of a book, more than one student can read and do a story map of the same book. This project allows you and the class members to appreciate students' understanding of books they have read.

How to Use the Activity

This activity can be used with individuals, pairs, or groups. Because this project is a variation of the mapping format, the format can be changed and modified before the assignment is given. The individual elements such as plot, protagonist, symbol, setting, mood, and theme can be taught through mini lessons because each term represents a unique and important concept by itself. Usually it is best if you first model the elements of fiction in a simpler form of literature, such as a short story. Decide on the size of the project; it should be put on a poster sheet that is large enough for a class presentation. The most beneficial part of this activity is that the poster will be shared with others and displayed in the classroom as an example of successful achievement.

Evaluation

This project can consist of several assessments. First, the accuracy and quality of the content can be evaluated as can the creativity, originality, and overall appearance of the poster itself. Second, the presentation can be graded in terms of speaking and sharing the visual with others. The audience can be required to take notes or write an interesting question or insight after viewing the project.

Variations

If computers are available, students can learn how to use them to enhance the appearance of the poster. They can experiment with different font styles and sizes. Graphics can be drawn or taken from clip art for symbols, settings, and characters. Placement, cutting and pasting, and layout are all important skills with this kind of format.

Of all the projects in this book, my students have commented repeatedly that they find this activity the most beneficial in helping them understand the important parts of every story.

Activity 25—Poster Story Map

Name: _____

Title: _____

Author: _____

Publisher and year: _____

Directions: Create a poster displaying important elements of the book. The poster should be large enough for all class members to view. Be creative, original, and colorful.

Main Character
Include the following:
- what he/she looks like
- 3 personality traits
- problems of character
- a picture of him/her

Plot
- a time ordered chart on the 5 main events of the plot
- the problem/conflict
- a 1-sentence summary

Print and Underline Title
Author and Publisher

Two New Vocabulary Words
- Print the word, copy the sentence from the book, and give the page number.
- Write the dictionary meaning of how it was used in the story.
- Write your own sentence.

Theme
- State the message or lesson in one sentence and explain it.

Symbol
- Draw or cut out a picture of an object that has a special meaning in the book.

Mood
- Complete the sentence: I felt _____ during the part in the story when

_____

_____ .

Activity 26—Book Jacket/Book Cover

Purpose of the Activity

This multipurpose activity involves students in reading, writing, representing a work in another medium, and viewing finished products in a sharing session. Students must first read a book and then create a book cover or book jacket that would advertise the book so that others will want to read it. Students must use higher-level thinking, analyzing, and creative skills in order to complete this assignment. After, the students will present their projects and share the information with the class. Also, they can talk about what elements are necessary to create a book cover or book jacket to market a book to readers.

How to Use the Activity

The activity, which should be assigned after the book is read, offers students a chance to express themselves in a format that they may not have explored in the past. Some class discussion about layout, attractiveness, and marketing may be necessary at the onset of the project. Having sample models of book covers and book jackets would be helpful. This activity provides the opportunity for mini lessons on summary writing, book reviews, symbolism, character descriptions, quotations, and any other information that you may request. Because the amount of space is limited on the cover/jacket, students work on writing with persuasion. Students can begin the project in class, or it can be assigned for homework. The cover or jacket can be cut to fit the actual book, or it can be made larger than the book for presentation purposes. You can assign a book cover alone or ask the entire class to contribute to a single book cover/jacket depending on how much information you want about the book.

Evaluation

Because this activity covers so many skills, it can be graded in a variety of ways. The students should be told exactly how they will be assessed. The writing and the literal and inferential information should be accurate. The design and attractiveness of the cover/jacket can be assessed on a rubric. Meeting a deadline is an important factor as well. If the project was done cooperatively, the cooperative group work can be considered. Finally, sharing with the class can be a separate grade.

Variations

Computer graphics and text can be incorporated into the cover/jacket. Also, students can draw on the cover/jacket themselves. Others can cut out pictures to represent ideas. You can use the ideas of creating book covers as a springboard for students' written work at any time.

Activity 26—Book Jacket/Book Cover

Name: _____ Date: _____

Title: _____

Author: _____

Publisher and year: _____

Directions: Create a book jacket/book cover as assigned following the format below. Look at sample book jackets and book covers in the library. Your project must contain information and be creative.

For the cover, do the following:

- Draw the characters and/or important objects from the book.
- Give the title, author, and publisher.

For the inside flaps of the jacket, do 4 of the following:

- Book review
- Author's background
- Important quotations
- Message of the book
- Opinion of other students
- Character descriptions

For the back cover, do the following:

- Give a short summary
- Explain why others should read the book

Activity 27—Comic Strip

Purpose of the Activity

This representing/viewing activity offers the opportunity for students to be creative and artistic as they display their understanding of an important event in the book. They will condense the events into a comic strip format and will explain, in writing, the message in the drawing. Additionally, the students will represent the literary form of the book in a different medium. If they share their work, their classmates will gain a deeper understanding of the book.

How to Use the Activity

This activity is most appropriate after reading the book, but the students can record significant events or situations in a journal as they read to refer to when they are done reading. They must then choose an event or situation to portray in a comic strip that they feel holds the most meaning for the book: a turning point, a character's decision, or an exciting plot event. You can set the parameters of the assignment and the number of comic strip frames as desired. You may want to use real comics from the newspaper to model in class and to use for discussion.

Evaluation

Because many students are not artistically inclined, stick figures should be accepted as people, and details may be sparse. Your assessment should be in the accuracy of the events portrayed and the reasoning for the choices of events. The interpretation is also a key element to consider in grading. Sharing in pairs, groups, or with the entire class can also be graded and can inspire class discussion and questions.

Variations

After students draw the comic strip individually, a group activity could be to ask students to share, discuss, and decide on the main idea for each comic strip together. Another possibility is to ask students to write the message of the story first and then draw a scene that best depicts that particular theme in a real-life situation at school.

Activity 27—Comic Strip

Name: _____ Date: _____

Title: _____

Author: _____

Publisher and year: _____

Directions: Choose an event that holds the most meaning for understanding your book for you. Some examples are a character's decision, a character solving a problem, or an action scene. Create a comic event with stick people to show others the scene with pictures.

Event	Event

Event	Event

Main Idea of the Strip

Event	Event	Main Idea of the Strip
Event	Event	

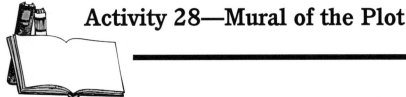

Activity 28—Mural of the Plot

Purpose of the Activity

There are several purposes for this representing/viewing activity. The first is for students to think at an interpretative level and show their understanding of the book with pictorial representations of characters and events. Second, the students must work cooperatively in order to successfully discuss the main events of the book, decide how to artistically create events in symbols, and complete the project on time to present it to the class as a visual. Third, students will present their mural to the class and explain the drawings, apply the symbols to life, and relate the significance of the events they portray to the book and its theme. The class will view the mural and listen in the share sessions to learn about the book(s) and their peers' interpretations.

How to Use the Activity

This activity can be assigned to a class reading the same book or to a class reading individual books. This activity can also be offered as one of several choices or projects from this book for students who like expressing themselves through art. Use butcher block paper for a larger version of a mural, or standard-size paper taped together to create a miniature wall hanging. The students must have an understanding of symbols, plot sequence, themes, and murals to undertake this activity. For younger children, concentrate on just the plot and the sequencing of events in pictures. Depending on your choices, mini lessons and modeling would be beneficial for project success by individuals. An art teacher can be a resource for ideas on artwork, the elements of a mural, and models. You need to decide the parameters of the assignment. Students can work in pairs, groups, or as an entire class if the class is small. The number of significant sections of the book must be discussed and outlined before the project begins. It is advisable for students to do sketches separately before doing a final copy. One possibility is to make sections on the mural by chapters, major episodes, or the events of the plot sequence.

Evaluation

The evaluation can include the preparation, working process, cooperative attitude, final product, and presentation. This project can be considered a formal activity, and each individual/pair/group can be held responsible for a particular part of the mural.

Variations

Once a class has completed a mural, keep it as a model if the project is repeated in the future. The mural's format can be thematic, sequential, chronological, a depiction of character growth, or a combination of the book's events paralleled with the actual historical events. The format for the mural depends on the structure of the book.

Activity 28—Mural of the Plot

Name: _____ Date:_____

Title: _____

Author: _____

Publisher and year: _____

Directions: Using the next page, create a wall mural displaying the plot by chapter or episodes. Use this smaller form to plan.

Activity 29—Author Promotion Poster

Purpose of the Activity

This activity involves students in reading, writing, researching, representing, and sharing. The audience is involved with viewing. Students can read one or more of an author's works and then research information about the author and his or her works. The students then will make a poster with important information about the author for class members to view. This activity reminds students that writers are real people with real lives.

How to Use the Activity

This activity will be most successful if all class members or groups are assigned individual writers to research and produce a poster to share. If class members are reading books of their choice, this project will be ideal for students to become familiar with many writers and types of literature. This project can also be used as a means for teaching the research and inquiry process, where the students write questions for which they would like answers. Students should look in a variety of sources in the library and, if available, use the World Wide Web. For younger children, you can bookmark specific sites to make the task easier and to focus their attention. For older children, students must gather and sort through materials to choose information about an author that answers their initial questions. Then they must be able to synthesize, condense, and write main ideas that are interesting and informative for a specific audience. The class members can log main ideas for each speaker in a notebook for future reference, which is also a form of notetaking practice. There are many possibilities for mini lessons on summarizing, paraphrasing, notetaking, finding main ideas, and researching.

Evaluation

The entire process can have several points for assessment as students participate in and complete the various steps of the research. If the students work independently, the final product can be graded. The class members' notes can be assessed after the presentations, and the importance of meeting a deadline should be stressed.

Variations

This activity can be offered as one of several projects for students to choose from as a book or author report. The format and information requested on the sample are only a model to get students started. When the project begins, the students can write their initial questions on the poster, and later they can explain how they arrived at their conclusions.

Activity 29—Author Promotion Poster

Name: _____ Date:_____

Title: _____

Author: _____

Publisher and year: _____

Directions: Create a poster about your book's author that includes the information below.

Background Information:
- Who is he/she? (if available)
- What is important to know?
- Where does he/she live?
- When did he/she write?
- Why is he/she successful?

Picture of Author

(If available)

Author's Name

Picture/Symbol for Author   **List of Other Books**

Explain, in 3 sentences, why you admire this author.

Activity 30—Mobile of Characters

Purpose of the Activity

The main purpose of this representing/viewing project is for students to display information about their book in a creative mobile that can be hung in the classroom. Students will learn about the characters in the book through the use of symbolic shapes and concise wording on each shape. Students must plan and prepare a project that is visually appealing as well as informative.

How to Use the Activity

This activity can be offered as one of several projects for students to choose from. Younger children and students who are creative, draw, and like a hands-on activity can choose to complete this assignment. The activity can also be used on a class book or several different books for variety. Students will need to pre-write with notes on several characters as they read to gather information or brainstorm after a reading to talk about the characters and their personalities. Because not all the information can be used in the predetermined amount of space, the students must be selective and choose the important facts that make a character different from others. You can direct the students to the kinds of information needed for character understanding. Using different shapes will help students realize that each character is unique in his or her own way. There should be a reason why a particular shape is chosen for a character. One side of the shape could be a picture, and the other side of the shape could contain written information about the character. You choose the size of the shapes and the type of paper. Students will punch holes in each shape and hang them from a coat hanger, rod, or piece of wood. Display the projects in the classroom for all students after sharing them formally or informally.

Evaluation

The project assessment can include the degree of creativity, the ability to meet a deadline, content, and a presentation.

Variations

This same idea could apply to the elements of fiction including plot, setting, mood, and themes for a book. Mobiles can also be used for vocabulary, symbols, and book reviews.

Activity 30—Mobile of Characters

Name: _____ Date: _____

Title: _____

Author: _____

Publisher and year: _____

Directions: Create a mobile based on the characters in the book you have read. Each character must have a picture or drawing to show your understanding of the character. On the other side, list some information (facts) about the character's life, family, personality, behavior, problems, friends, and other items of interest. These shapes can be cut out and attached to a coat hanger. The pieces can hang from string, ribbon, or strips of material.

Be prepared to share your project with the class.

Name of Characters—Boy or Girl—What do you remember that makes him/her different in the book?

1.

2.

3.

4.

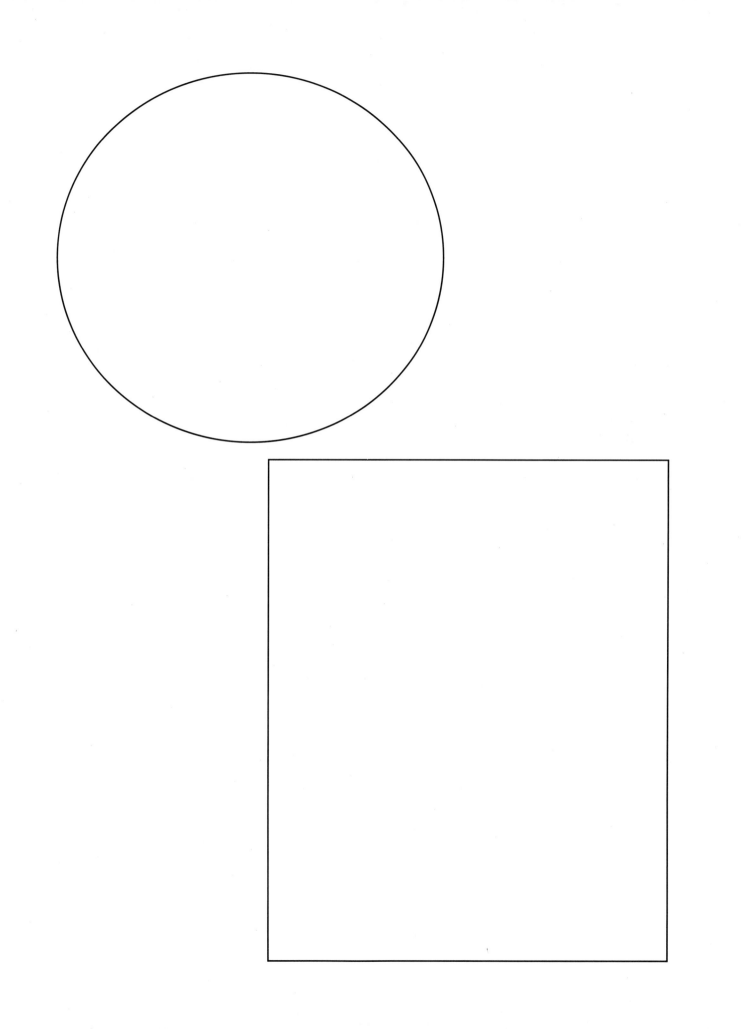

Activity 31—Award Certificate

Purpose of the Activity

The purpose of this representing/viewing activity is for students to analytically decide which character from a book deserves an award certificate for heroic traits. Students must create an award stating both literal and inferential information. Another purpose of this activity is for students to express themselves in writing by giving reasons to justify their candidate choices. Upon presenting the award for class members to view, students will discuss the idea of a hero and heroic traits. Students are learning persuasive writing by writing to convince the audience that their character deserves an award.

How to Use the Activity

The award activity can be used as a model for students so that they can create their own award with whatever design they feel is appropriate. This topic lends itself to a discussion on heroism. Everyday behavior of doing "good deeds" for others can be awarded as well as grand scale acts of saving people in dangerous situations. For pre-writing students can brainstorm examples from their own lives and the everyday world. The writing process including rough draft writing, editing, and publishing a final draft can be practiced through the explanation of the award.

Evaluation

Students can be assessed on their writing process work and on the final product. A formal persuasive speech can also be set up for evaluation, or informal sharing can be done in groups or pairs.

Variations

Students can create awards for characters for different reasons. Students can create other kinds of awards for characters in their books, such as "Best Friend Award," "Best Parent Award," or "Best Problem Solver." Younger children may enjoy voting for the best awards for characters in the books that they have read.

Activity 31—Award Certificate

Name: _____ Date:_____

Title: _____

Author: _____

Publisher and year: _____

Directions: Create an award for a character in your book. Think of a quality or deed for which your character deserves an award. Complete the section below to explain the reasons why this person should receive an award. Make sure you give specific examples from the book. Write in complete sentences.

Name of person receiving the award: _____

List 3 descriptive words for this person:

1. _____

2. _____

3. _____

Title of award: _____

Reasons for award: _____

_____

_____

_____

_____

Awarded to

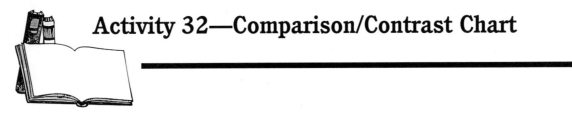

Activity 32—Comparison/Contrast Chart

Purpose of the Activity

There are several purposes for this representing/viewing activity. It gives students the opportunity to write, to represent their knowledge in a chart, and to have their classmates view their projects. Students will use higher-level thinking skills to compare and contrast one character to another and/or themselves. By studying similarities and differences between characters, students will understand the many differences and similarities among people. This can open a discussion about empathy for people and their problems. Students will present and share their information either formally or informally with class members. Finally, the class will view a chart and listen to their peers' ideas.

How to Use the Activity

This activity can be used for the entire class, or it can be offered as one choice of several activities. Students can complete this activity during reading or afterward. The activity requires the students to look beyond the text for similarities and differences. Modeling in class with concrete examples first will increase understanding. For younger children, a list of descriptive vocabulary words that students could manipulate for character comparison would make this activity more successful. Students need to find specific examples to support their generalizations and observations. The graphic organizer can be used as a rough draft. A final draft can become a larger visual for the presentation, if students are to practice presentation skills. Some elements for comparison include personality, parents, hobbies, interests, schooling, problems, appearance, background, friends, relationships, and likes and dislikes.

Evaluation

This activity can be evaluated in a number of ways. It can be assessed as a class or homework activity, a written assignment, or a presentation. The amount of credit given for an assignment depends on the time and purpose of the project.

Variations

Students can create their own charts for comparisons and contrasts between two minor characters, two books, or two elements within a book. These charts can also be used as graphic organizers to help students pre-write before a formal writing project is assigned. A column on the reproducible can be changed on the chart and the student's name can be added so that a character's trait can be compared and contrasted to a real person.

Activity 32—Comparison/Contrast Chart

Name: _____ Date:_____

Title: _____

Author: _____

Publisher and year: _____

Directions: Create a chart to share with the class that compares similarities and contrasts differences for two characters in your book. Write an example from the book to help explain your answer.

Item Discussed	Same or Different	First Character's Name	Second Character's Name	Example from Book
1.				
2.				
3.				

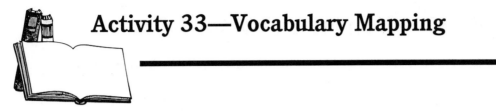

Activity 33—Vocabulary Mapping

Purpose of the Activity

The first purpose for this activity is to have students increase their vocabulary by interacting with new words in context. The second purpose is for the students to assume responsibility for their learning by choosing words that they are unfamiliar with as they read. Third, students will learn from each other by presentations of words in class. Fourth, students will practice thinking symbolically to help increase memory and to help them make connections to their lives.

How to Use the Activity

There are several ways to use this graphic organizer. One is for students to find a certain number of words to map as they read. You can pass out the required number of forms to the students for mapping. Another suggestion, especially for younger children, is for each student to find and share one word for class members to write down, thus creating a class list of vocabulary enhancement. This form can also be used as a model for students to use for a poster presentation on their vocabulary word.

Evaluation

Students can be assessed on their ability to meet a deadline, to create a word map with accurate information, and to share information by practicing their presentation skills. One method of testing a group of class vocabulary words is for you to use the students' sentences for a quiz and ask students to match a list of words with the correct blanks in the sentences. Students will need to use contextual skills to choose which vocabulary word makes sense in each sentence. Another form of testing includes using just the student-drawn pictures for matching with the class vocabulary words.

Variations

You can vary the requested information on a word if you are stressing antonyms, homonyms, etymology, or dictionary skills. You can also request that the students use a number of vocabulary words in a specific writing assignment or one of the suggested activity book projects. The more exposure students have to the vocabulary, the more likely the words will become part of their everyday language.

Activity 33—Vocabulary Mapping

Name: _____ Date: _____

Title: _____

Author: _____

Publisher and year: _____

Write the Dictionary Definition   **Write Your Own Sentence**

_____   _____

_____   _____

_____   _____

Write the Word

_____

Sentence from Book

_____

Page Number from Book

_____

Part of Speech

_____

Write Two Synonyms   **Draw a Picture to Remember the Word**

_____

_____

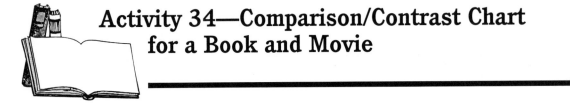

Activity 34—Comparison/Contrast Chart for a Book and Movie

Purpose of the Activity

First, the students must read a book and watch the movie version of it. Then the students must record information in a chart that requires familiarity with specific terms. This activity has students using higher-level thinking skills to compare and contrast specific points and deciding whether the two media are similar to or different from each other and how. The students will make judgments and support their answers and choices. They will discuss their choices after reading and viewing the two media.

How to Use the Activity

The students can complete the chart while they read, or all three columns can be completed after reading the book and viewing the movie. This activity would work successfully with groups, pairs, or individuals depending on the ability and maturity of the group and your purpose. One advantage of having students work cooperatively is that they can be given roles for which they are responsible and a specific task to complete. Members should share openly but be dependent on each other for the success of the task. Some possible roles are organizer, recorder, reporter, and timekeeper.

There may be a need for background information on different types of genres and some of the terms asked for in the chart. Model as much as possible, possibly with a children's book like *The Velveteen Rabbit*. Often, both books and movies can be obtained from the library.

Evaluation

Students can be assessed for their observations and analyses of the two art forms. By allowing cooperative grouping, you may be increasing success for students who are less observant or insightful. This activity can be graded as a class assignment, formal written report, or graphic organizer presentation. The main focus should be that students explain with details the reasons for their answers.

Variations

Alter the form to emphasize whatever points you feel are necessary. For younger children you may want to work on similarities or differences only for one particular lesson. The chart could be used for two books of a genre or author as well.

Activity 34—Comparison/Contrast Chart for a Book and Movie

Name: _____ Date: _____

Title: _____

Author: _____

Publisher and year: _____

Directions: If your book is also a movie, you can complete the chart below and write how the two are the same or different. 1 = Low; 5 = High

Item Discussed	Name of Book	Name of Movie	Similar or Different and How?
Events in Story			
Main Character			
Where and When the Story Takes Place			
Main Problems in Story			
Rating in Stars and Why			

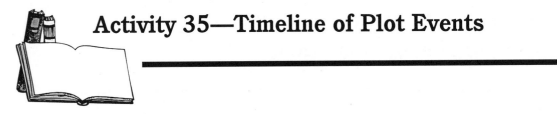

Activity 35—Timeline of Plot Events

Purpose of the Activity

The purpose of this activity is for students to choose important events from the book and arrange them in sequential order using words and/or symbolic pictures. The students must also explain the significance of the events and reasons why they were chosen for the timeline. The students will represent the book in a format that requires them to use higher thinking skills in order to analyze, find, and sequentially arrange objects to represent actions in the book. The students will share their timelines with the class for discussion. Creating and understanding patterns in the text increases comprehension.

How to Use the Activity

Students can keep a journal as they read so that they can record important events and significant symbolism. Then they can use their notes to choose the most important events that cover the plot from the beginning to the end. Keep in mind that younger children may be able to concentrate only on sequence, while older children may be able to think abstractly with symbolic representations. The events should be labeled below the horizontal timeline with concise words. Above the timeline, the students should draw or place pictorial symbols that represent each event in the sequence of the plot. Students can write, orally present, or both and share with the class their choices as well as the significance of the events in the book.

Evaluation

Depending on what you choose to focus on with this activity, the students can be evaluated for their sequencing skills, writing skills, content information, or speaking skills or on all four. The students must be aware of the emphasis at the beginning of the project.

Variations

Enlarge the timeline so students can create a visual for class presentation. You can also increase or decrease the number of events requested on the timeline. A possible pre-writing activity is for students to practice working with timelines by placing important events in their lives in sequence and bringing symbolic objects that represent those moments in their lives.

A mini lesson that enhances understanding of patterns of text is to have students look for transitional words that signal sequence and time order in writing. Students can highlight, circle, or write down the words from stories that they read.

Activity 35—Timeline of Plot Events

Name: _____ Date: _____

Title: _____

Author: _____

Publisher and year: _____

Directions: Create a timeline of events in your book. Use words below the line and pictures above the line to show the actions. Be ready to explain your choices. Use this page to plan. Use the larger timeline page for your final copy.

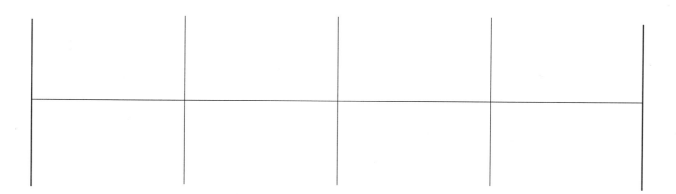

Activity 36—Travel Brochure

Purpose of the Activity

This activity emphasizes representing/viewing standards. Students should be original and imaginative in creating a brochure about a setting (fictional or real) used in a book. They will need to view professional travel books and brochures to get ideas for their own projects, and they will need to research the settings to find accurate information to include in their brochures. Students will share their projects with their classmates and increase their knowledge of the book.

How to Use the Activity

This activity can be assigned to an entire class or offered as one of several choices. Artistic students often find this a golden opportunity to display their learning style. Because some prior knowledge about travel brochure formats, places in the world, and art layout is necessary, students should research the settings used in their book. The use of the Internet, travel books from the library, or interviews with people in the travel business could be made available to them. Students can brainstorm the kind of information needed to make a travel brochure attractive to customers. They should plan their designs before drawing and writing. Using a computer with a program wizard or different fonts and graphics would make the brochures attractive, and students would become acquainted with desktop publishing. Drawn or cutout pictures are equally acceptable. When the project is done, the students can share their work formally in a presentation or informally in groups. They can also explain the reasons the author chose a particular setting for the book.

Evaluation

This project can be assessed in stages. The research and preliminary planning process can be evaluated as can the final product. Students can assess each other's brochures by deciding which places they would like to visit and their reasons for choosing those places.

Variations

Students can be given a specific format to follow or a certain setting to promote if they need more structure. Students can also practice writing business letters to travel bureaus to request information on a particular place. There are also toll-free phone numbers for every state. They can use the information for the brochure and expand their background knowledge of the book.

Activity 36—Travel Brochure

Name: _____ Date: _____

Title: _____

Author: _____

Publisher and year: _____

Directions: Create a travel brochure explaining the setting, the where and when, used in the book. Make it colorful and include important information.

Where: _____ **When:** _____

Activity 37—Postcard

Purpose of the Activity

There are several purposes for this activity, which involves reading, writing, representing, and viewing. First, the students must read a book and understand a character well enough to assume the identity of that character and write a postcard to another character in the story. Second, the students will use their writing skills to concisely communicate some ideas about significant actions, decisions, and/or observations in the book. Third, the students will represent the book in another form that displays their interpretations of character and plot. Fourth, the class members will view each other's work to gain more insight into the characters and the thought processes of other students.

How to Use the Activity

You can assign this project to a class or offer it as one of several to choose from for a book project. Show the class sample postcards for models and discuss reasons why people communicate in this manner. Large index cards would allow students to draw a picture of a setting or an event from the plot from the book and use the other side for the message and address. The form for the postcard (page 86) can be enlarged if the emphasis is only on writing or if more space is needed for younger children. After students produce the postcards, they can share them with classmates and explain the significance of the communication in relation to the book.

Evaluation

Students can be evaluated for the written portion of the project (the message), for following the directions and format properly, for maintaining accuracy of details, for meeting a deadline, for being creative, and for sharing the project with others.

Variations

To help direct students, you can suggest the message topic or offer several choices for students. You can also dictate which character is writing to which other character.

Activity 37—Postcard

Name: _____ Date: _____

Title: _____

Author: _____

Publisher and year: _____

Directions: Imagining that you are one of the characters from your book, write a postcard to another character in your book. Think about something that might be important to your character, a problem, or something that he or she learned.

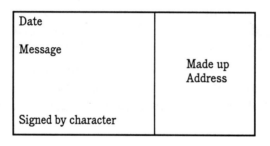

Activity 38—Bumper Sticker

Purpose of the Activity

There are several purposes for this activity. The most important one is that the students will pass along positive themes, inspiring motifs, or words of wisdom from a book in the form of a bumper sticker. The students must brainstorm before actually writing their message in a concise, clear manner. Then the students must defend their choices with examples from the text and apply their messages to the real world. When students can make connections to their lives and the world around them, more processing of information into long-term memory takes place and comprehension is increased. Finally, students will present their bumper stickers to the class.

How to Use the Activity

In this activity, students are asked to brainstorm universal themes or messages from the book. Discuss the purpose of a bumper sticker, and show sample bumper stickers so the students can get a better idea about this form of communication. The students must select the best saying or theme that is appropriate for a bumper sticker. Word choice and sentence length are important factors so a mini lesson on use of a thesaurus and sentence writing may be appropriate. Another factor is to remind students that the message should affect viewers positively. After pre-writing, they will place the saying on a bumper sticker and decorate it. Additionally, they must explain in writing the significance of the insight for their book and why the message is universal. These bumper stickers can be laminated and put on a bulletin board, or they can be magnetized for display on a blackboard. The students can share in groups or with the entire class.

Evaluation

This project can be evaluated in terms of students' abilities to meet a deadline, complete an assignment, follow directions, be creative, explain the message as it relates to the book and life, and present the project in a clear manner.

Variations

Students can discuss other forms of communication that people use to get ideas across in public places. They can also choose a bumper sticker from the class's presentations and write about how it applies to their lives.

Younger children might like making a game out of the bumper stickers if several books are involved by trying to match the messages with the books that were read.

Activity 38—Bumper Sticker

Name: _____ Date:_____

Title: _____

Author: _____

Publisher and year: _____

Directions: Think of a clever message that you learned from your book that you could put on a bumper sticker for others to read. Explain in 3 sentences why you chose this message. Use the next page to design your bumper sticker.

Explain:

_____

_____

_____

_____

_____

_____

_____

_____

_____

_____

_____

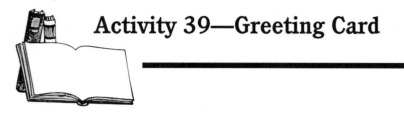

Activity 39—Greeting Card

Purpose of the Activity

This representing/viewing/writing activity has students assuming the identity of a character in order to write a greeting card to another character. Students must first understand the variety of reasons why people write and send cards to one another. Then the students must choose a specific purpose, decide on characters, and find a situation in the book where one character might have sent a card to another. The students will make assumptions, based on facts and events in the book, about how sending the card would have changed the plot, and they will write their explanation with supporting details from the text. Finally, the class members will view all the cards, listen to the explanations, and share their interpretations.

How to Use the Activity

This post-reading project is most successfully completed individually. Allow students time to preview a variety of greeting cards and discuss the kinds of cards that they might have received. A discussion of types of cards and their purposes will also connect prior knowledge to the project. You can ask students to pre-write about several situations, character relationships, and critical decision points in the book that may lend themselves to this form of communication. Students can also discuss letters, cards, or other communications that have effected their lives. The form on page 92 can be used for students to write on directly, or pieces of paper can be folded in half to create any number of cards. Also there are "publisher" computer programs containing clipart that allow students to create cards. Students enjoy and learn by sharing each other's projects in class, either formally or informally.

Evaluation

This project can be graded by fulfilling the greeting card requirements and the written explanation of the card's relationship to the characters and events in the book. Students could also be given a grade for sharing, if you require a formal presentation.

Variations

Ask students to respond to the greeting card in some way. They can also make judgments about whether the various cards would actually have effected a character's decisions or the plot events. They can rank cards according to their appropriateness and effectiveness.

Activity 39—Greeting Card

Name: _____ Date: _____

Title: _____

Author: _____

Publisher and year: _____

Directions: Choose a reason to send a card from one character to another in your book. Create a card with a cover and a message. Then explain why you chose this type of card. Some card types are: Birthday, Thank You, Get Well, Friendship, Missing You.

Choice of card: _____

From: _____   To: _____

(Front)   **(Inside)**

Activity 40—Fortune Cookie Sayings

Purpose of the Activity

In this representing/viewing activity, students must write a concise message for each important character that would be appropriate according to their past, present, or future life. Thus, the purposes of the activity are for students to display understanding of characters, to make inferences based on details and facts from the book, to write concisely, to be creative, and to have fun. This activity also gives students the opportunity to share or present their work so classmates can learn from it.

How to Use the Activity

This activity can be used as a post-reading project for a class book or individually chosen books. If the term "fortune cookie" is not generally known to the students, you can explain it. Bring actual fortune cookies to class as examples. Students can use the real fortunes as models or even match them with characters from books.

Evaluation

The assessment depends on the emphasis that you want to place on the activity. This activity can be used as a class activity or as an individual book project. Students can make a presentation on one or more of the fortunes and offer an extensive explanation for matching a fortune with a character.

Variations

Have the students randomly choose a fortune from a hat, match it to a character in the book if possible, and explain why the fortune matches that particular character or why it doesn't match any character. The fortunes can also be used for writing for an extensive composition later.

Activity 40—Fortune Cookie Sayings

Name: _____ Date: _____

Title: _____

Author: _____

Publisher and year: _____

Directions: Write a prediction or saying for each main character in your book. Then explain why you wrote the message.

```
┌──────────────────────────────────────────────────┐
│ Fortune 1                                          │
│                                                    │
│                                                    │
│                                                    │
└──────────────────────────────────────────────────┘
```

Character's name and your explanation

_____

_____

```
┌──────────────────────────────────────────────────┐
│ Fortune 2                                          │
│                                                    │
│                                                    │
│                                                    │
└──────────────────────────────────────────────────┘
```

Character's name and your explanation

_____

_____

```
┌──────────────────────────────────────────────────┐
│ Fortune 3                                          │
│                                                    │
│                                                    │
│                                                    │
└──────────────────────────────────────────────────┘
```

Character's name and your explanation

_____

_____

Part III

Speaking and Listening Standards Activities

Activity 41—Tell Me About Your Book

Purpose of the Activity

This activity emphasizes speaking and listening skills that will give students the opportunity to share their knowledge of a book with class members. Other students will learn about new titles and authors that they might want to sample. Because all the students are members of the audience, they can practice appropriate listening skills by being courteous, attentive, and supportive during the book talks. Finally, students will sharpen their speaking skills in front of an audience.

How to Use the Activity

This activity can be used when a class reads a variety of books and individuals have presentations to share. You might just want the class to get an overview of the books to enhance understanding. Usually all class members can share their books within one or two class periods. Students can refer to note cards or the reproducible but should not be allowed to simply read the information to the class. Generally, students find this book talk format less threatening than longer speeches, and they are often eager to present their projects in this manner if a written project is also due. For younger children, this activity introduces them to giving speeches to classmates.

Evaluation

Because this activity is an informal sharing of information about a book, you may want to grade the speech informally by giving credit for sharing and following the directions or no credit for being unprepared or unwilling to share. Students worry less if the emphasis is not on the speech but on the willingness to share a book with others.

Variations

Students can sit in a circle to share if the class is small or can form several small groups if the class is large. You can vary the information that is asked for in the book talk. If book talks are used often, students become familiar with speaking with the class, which prepares them for more formal presentations later.

Activity 41—Tell Me About Your Book

Name: _____ Date:_____

Title: _____

Author: _____

Publisher and year: _____

Suggestions for Book Sharing:
1. Hold up the book for the class members to view and name the title, author, publisher, and year of publication of the book.

2. To give an overview of the story, tell a short summary of the events of the plot using about five sentences.

   _____

   _____

   _____

   _____

   _____

3. Describe the main character by using four adjectives, and tell whether you would like him or her as a friend. Why or why not?

   _____   _____

   _____   _____

4. Explain something you learned from the book and give reasons why you liked or disliked the book.

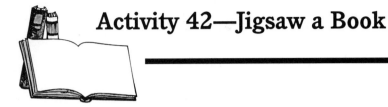

Activity 42—Jigsaw a Book

Purpose of the Activity

This activity involves listening and speaking standards. Its purpose is for students to work cooperatively to read a portion of a book and share information to create a basic familiarity with the characters and plot among all class members. Hopefully, students will become interested enough to read the book in its entirety, or even another title by the same author. This jigsaw activity is also a motivational one for students who think they cannot read an entire book; here, they can cover an entire book in a few days.

How to Use the Activity

The directions are stated on the activity sheet. This activity can also be used as a motivational activity to begin a novel unit, to introduce a genre type, to add variety when teaching about an author, or to teach plot structure. The students are always surprised that a teacher would assign only a few pages to each student. With older students and longer chapter books, you could also tear up parts or chapters and pass them out; this action certainly gets their attention! The chapters can be stapled and saved for reuse after the activity is over. You must be prepared to speak about parts or chapters when students are absent or unprepared so that the plot flows in sequence. There can be no makeup for students in this type of activity.

Steps to Follow

Choose a book that has enough chapters for all students or for students to work in pairs or groups. The book must be readable by all class members. Assign the pages or tear the book into chapters. For effect and to stress the need to save time, you may want to tear the chapters in front of the class. Read the first and possibly the second chapter to the class out loud. Give each student or group a chapter and the table of contents. Have the students read their chapters and take notes as stated on the activity sheet. If possible, the students should get in a circle and talk about their parts. Everyone should listen without interrupting. For older students, you may request that students take notes on plot events and characters. Read the last chapter or two aloud upon completion of the sharing to add closure to the activity. Lastly, have students write a summary of the plot based on what they heard. They should discuss and evaluate the process of reading a book in this fashion.

Evaluation

The assessment can take into consideration the students' ability to follow directions, share information, and listen to or take notes on what other students share. Evaluation of the summary writing and critiquing of the activity can take place at the conclusion of the sharing.

Variations

The amount of information requested can be lengthened depending on the time you want to allow for the presentations. Remember, the longer the sharing goes on, the higher the risk of students being absent and being unable to follow the plot sequence.

Activity 42—Jigsaw a Book

_____

Name: _____ Date:_____

Title: _____

Author: _____

Publisher and year: _____

Directions: We will read the book as a class with everyone working together to read a portion of the book and help everyone understand their part.

- Once you have received your pages, read them, and answer the questions below.
- Share your answers with your group.
- When someone is talking, listen without interrupting.
- After everyone in your group has shared their information, write a summary of the plot.

Guidelines for notetaking on each chapter

1. What happened in the pages you read? Were any new characters introduced?

2. What do think is going to happen in the next several pages?

3. What questions would you like answered in later chapters?

Write a summary here.

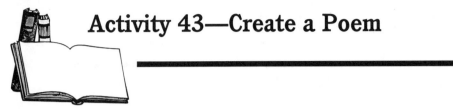

Activity 43—Create a Poem

Purpose of the Activity

This creative writing activity involves the reading of a book and the writing of poetry and has students share their ideas and feelings with other class members. This project covers the standards of reading, writing, speaking, and listening. The students also learn new forms of poetry, and they must make connections between poetry and prose by writing about universal themes and feelings.

How to Use the Activity

This post-reading activity will be most successful if students work individually to express their feelings and relate their own experiences to the book and their poems. This activity can also be used in conjunction with a poetry unit. Students need to see similarities between the themes of different genres. You can assign this activity to students who have all read the same book or who have read individual books. The activity can be offered as one of several projects from this book for students to choose according to their learning strengths. For younger children, you may choose to teach only one type of poetry.

Evaluation

This activity can be assessed as other writing and sharing projects are assessed. Grades can be given for the writing portion and for the speaking/sharing portion. Other factors to consider are the ability to meet a deadline, to follow directions, to format the poems correctly, and to explain the theme and its relationship to the book and poems.

Variations

The students can illustrate their poems and create a visual aid for their presentation. You can choose how many and what kinds of poems are required for the project. There are many more types of poems the students could try than the ones suggested, which were chosen because they are short, fun, and have easy formats to follow. It might be helpful for students to browse through children's books of poetry either in the classroom or the library for examples and ideas.

Activity 43—Create a Poem

Name: _____ Date:_____

Title: _____

Author: _____

Publisher and year: _____

Directions: Write a poem about your book. Focus on a feeling, a character, setting, or plot.

Message from book:_____

_____

_____ .

_____

Poem Suggestions: Haiku, Limerick, Cinquain, or Free Verse

Haiku   Title: _____

    Line 1: 5 syllables
    Line 2: 7 syllables
    Line 3: 5 syllables

_____

_____

_____

Limerick   Title: _____

       Line 1: A
       Line 2: A
       Line 3: B
       Line 4: B
       Line 5: A

Lines 1, 2, and 5 rhyme. Lines 3 and 4 are usually shorter.

_____

_____

_____

_____

_____

Cinquain   Title: _____

       Line 1: 1 word (a noun—thing)
       Line 2: 2 words (adjectives—words that tell what kind, how many,
              or which one)
       Line 3: 3 words (verbs—words that show action)
       Line 4: 4 words (a phrase about the noun)
       Line 5: 5 words (a synonym for the noun)

_____

_____

_____

_____

_____

Free Verse   Title: _____

This type of poetry does not contain rhyme or any particular pattern. Be precise choosing specific sensory images.

_____

_____

_____

_____

_____

_____

_____

Activity 44—Create a Song

Purpose of Activity

This reading/writing/speaking/listening activity allows students to display their creative talents by writing lyrics for a song based on a character or an incident from a book. Students will learn the difficult process of writing words that connect with music. The more connections that the students can make between the characters and/or the plot to their own lives, the more understanding the students will have about the book and themselves. They must also share their ideas and feelings with others so they can practice speaking and presentational skills. The audience members can practice their listening skills. Both speakers and listeners learn to appreciate each other.

How to Use the Activity

This post-reading activity can be worked on individually or in pairs. You can decide how many lines and/or stanzas there should be and how long they are. Students can discuss creative artists and the process of writing lyrics and music. Some students may already be familiar with writing music and playing instruments and can share their insights. Because some students may feel uncomfortable about writing lyrics if they do not like music, this activity can be offered as one of several to choose from. For older students in particular, sample songs can be played in class so the students can discuss the messages and feelings expressed in music.

Evaluation

Although this activity involves writing, the primary emphasis is on the presentation of the lyrics to the class. The students should understand the assessment process (as defined by you) at the beginning of the assignment. A major consideration is the connection between the lyrics and the book.

Variations

Ask students to bring songs that have a similar character, plot, theme, or feeling to the book under discussion, and have the students explain the connections of the songs and book to their own lives.

Activity 44—Create a Song

Name: _____ Date:_____

Title: _____

Author: _____

Publisher and year: _____

Directions: Write a song about a character or incident in your book. Be prepared to share your project with the class.

Write the character or incident the song is about: _____

_____

Name of song: _____

Music: _____

Words: _____

_____

_____

_____

_____

_____

_____

_____

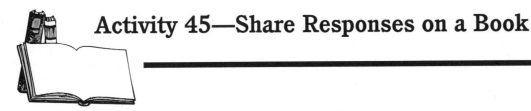

Activity 45—Share Responses on a Book

Purpose of the Activity

The purpose of this activity is for students to read, write, speak, and listen interactively with the text as well as with each other in class. This cooperative activity asks students to make connections during or after the reading by having students write notes and questions. Then they must interact with their classmates and respond to one another's questions to help make the text more understandable for each other. By having the students read through the questions, evaluate, and make judgments as well as respond aloud, students are using higher-level thinking skills. The other students will listen and gain further insights into the book.

How to Use the Activity

Class members will write three questions or comments on index cards (or on three slips of paper cut from the worksheet) while they are reading their book or immediately after they finish reading. It is important that the teacher model the type of questions to ask. For younger children, question stems could be displayed on the board such as "In your opinion...," "At what point did you like or not like the story?," and "Is the ending believable?," are some examples of question stems. Students should put their name on each card to receive credit for participating and to add validity to the types of questions and comments that will be asked on the cards. (Students should be familiar with journal or response writing prior to this activity.) The students' cards are shuffled and distributed randomly to class members, who will read the questions and the names of the persons who wrote the questions. Then the classmate will answer his or her three questions in the form of a response on the cards and sign his or her name. The students can work in pairs or groups sharing their responses. The students then choose the most valuable question and response to read aloud to the class. These responses can be used for further discussion if you so desire. By having the students perform these tasks, they are creating their own study guide on the book, making personal connections, and taking responsibility for their learning. All students are given the opportunity to ask questions and get answers. This activity can be repeated more than once during the reading of a longer book. Decide how much time should be spent on the questions.

Evaluation

This project can be counted as a class participation activity and thus part of a daily grade. If students are to write more detailed responses, it can be considered a writing assignment. The main purpose, however, is to get the students to talk and share information with each other.

Variations

Instead of passing the questions randomly among the students for classmates to answer, students can write their own questions and answer the questions themselves. Another possibility for younger students is to be more structured and post questions on the board for students to choose from to write down and answer on the cards. You can still pass the cards around for discussion.

Activity 45—Share Responses on a Book

Name: _____ Date: _____

Title: _____

Author: _____

Publisher and year: _____

Directions: Write three questions either on this sheet or on index cards concerning plot, characters, problems, or unusual ideas. You will respond to three other students' questions after the cards are collected and passed out again.

Question 1: _____

_____

Name of person who wrote the question: _____

Response: _____

_____

Name of person who is responding: _____

Question 2: _____

_____

Name of person who wrote the question: _____

Response: _____

_____

Name of person who is responding: _____

Question 3: _____

_____

Name of person who wrote the question: _____

Response: _____

_____

Name of person who is responding: _____

Activity 46—Your Favorite Part of the Book

Purpose of the Activity

This activity focuses primarily on reading, speaking, and listening skills. The students must choose a passage from their book that has a special meaning to them. Then they must practice reading the passage several times both silently and orally to practice fluency before reading it to the class in the form of a presentation. The students must also write and say the reasons why they chose that particular passage. The audience must practice active listening skills and learn to be nonjudgmental and to respect their peers' opinions.

How to Use the Activity

This activity involves discussion of the skills necessary and important for a good oral interpretation and fluency in reading. You should model the difference between reading silently for yourself and reading out loud for an audience. The listening skills expected by the audience need to be discussed in class before the presentations begin. By having the students practice their reading silently first, the students can pay close attention to vocabulary, sentence structure, and punctuation. When they practice out loud, the students get used to hearing their own voices and can work on timing and oral fluency. Lastly, by practicing with a partner, the students learn to work cooperatively and practice listening and possibly critiquing skills. You may want to approve the passages first by using the activity worksheet. The length and duration of the passage will be set by you.

Evaluation

Both the speakers and listeners may be assessed depending on the maturity of the group. A rubric can be devised to cover the skills being developed. Clarity, volume, speed, eye contact, preparation, time limits, and introductions and explanations are factors to consider. For the audience, paying attention, not talking, not being a distraction, sitting forward, focusing, taking notes (if requested), and responding appropriately could be part of the grade.

Variations

Depending on the level of the group, the students can memorize short passages or poems for their presentations.

Activity 46—Your Favorite Part of the Book

Name: _____ Date:_____

Title: _____

Author: _____

Publisher and year: _____

Directions: Find your favorite part of your book to share with the class. Be prepared to read the passage to the class and explain why you chose it. The length of the passage should be 1–3 paragraphs.

Page number of the passage: _____

Explain why you chose this passage:

_____

_____

_____

_____

_____

Points to remember when reading aloud for the class:
1. Practice the passage silently at least 2 times watching for unusual words and punctuation.
2. Practice the passage out loud by yourself. Speak slowly, clearly, and with expression.
3. Practice with a partner for confidence.

Activity 47—Share a Vocabulary Word

Purpose of the Activity

There are four purposes for this activity. The first is to increase the vocabulary of the students by having them choose their own words and teach the words to each other. Secondly, through class presentations, the students will practice their speaking skills in front of an audience, relating planned, practiced, and practical information that all classmates need to know to understand the word. Thirdly, the class members will practice their listening and notetaking skills during the presentation, writing down information on the words that they could possibly use in a later activity. Fourthly, the students will act appropriately as an audience.

How to Use the Activity

Assign this activity when the students start their books, so they can look for a word to share as they read. While the books are read or being taught, you can spread out the presentations to coincide with the discussion of particular pages or chapters in class. A date column is included for students to keep track of presentations. If no more than three or four words are presented at a time, the class time used for this activity is kept to a minimum, and other activities can be planned. You must request that the students take notes, listen attentively, and use the words in future assignments. You might ask students to use the words in compositions and highlight their presence for extra points. The memory aid brought by the students can be objects, actions, or something drawn or written on the chalkboard. These concrete examples will help the audience retain the knowledge of the words.

Evaluation

This activity can be evaluated on several bases: meeting a deadline, following directions for teaching the vocabulary word, content, speaking skills, and audience skills (cooperation, attentiveness, notetaking, and behavior). Comprehension and memory of new words is increased when they are used more often.

Variations

Create a list of words necessary for comprehension of the book. Assign each student or pair of students a word. The reproducible can be used as a note-taking sheet and/or study guide. Alter the sheet as necessary.

Activity 47—Share a Vocabulary Word

Name: _____ Date: _____

Title: _____

Author: _____

Publisher and year: _____

Directions: Each class member will sign up to present an interesting or unusual vocabulary word from their reading. Class members must take notes on all the words. You will be assigned a date to present your word to the class. You are to teach your word to the class. Bring a picture, personal story, or prop to help everyone remember and understand your word.

Information Required:
1. Page number the word appears on in the book
2. The sentence from the book with the word underlined
3. A definition that matches the use of the word in the book
4. The part of speech
5. Your own sentence with the word underlined

Class List of Shared Words:

	Name	Page Number	Date	Word	Definition
1.					
2.					
3.					

Name	Page Number	Date	Word	Definition
4.				
5.				
6.				
7.				
8.				
9.				
10.				
11.				
12.				
13.				
14.				

Name	Page Number	Date	Word	Definition
15.				
16.				
17.				
18.				
19.				
20.				
21.				
22.				
23.				
24.				
25.				

Activity 48—Panel Discussion on a Book

Purpose of the Activity

The main purpose of this speaking/listening activity is for students to practice impromptu speaking by presenting their opinions and points of view on a topic and to also practice listening to their peers' opinions without criticizing. Students must think about a question, organize their thoughts, verbalize their opinions, support their responses with examples, and work with others to draw conclusions. The last part of the activity is to increase comprehension by discussing in a cooperative setting and recording new ideas.

How to Use the Activity

The students can be divided into groups of at least four students per group for several panel discussions. If different students are reading a variety of titles for literature circles, the groups are already formed. If everyone is reading the same book, then it is your decision how to form groups. You could ask the students to write the topics and questions and choose the best ones. You could use Activity 57 from this book, or you could be very direct with areas in the book that you want to reinforce. If your purpose is to increase student involvement and teach good questioning techniques, then you will want students to write the questions. By reproducing pages, cutting out the questions, and placing them in a hat, you can save some time. Make sure that you preview the questions before placing them in the hat. The discussion should be informal, with the student panel seated at a table or at desks facing the class members. Each member should pull one topic or question and be allowed to finish before questions or comments from the audience are allowed. At the end of all the panels, time can be given for students to discuss in their groups some conclusions about the book, new insights, or different opinions.

Evaluation

This activity can receive as much credit as other book projects. At the beginning of the activity, the students need to know the criteria being used for evaluation. The panel members can be graded individually for their participation in the panel and on their ability to support their opinions with examples from the text. Other assessments can be for completing the panel sheet, working in a group, and taking turns speaking and listening. You can assess the audience's skills as they ask more questions and listen to the speakers.

Variations

A variation of the panel discussion is to use this activity after presentations of other projects for students to learn about other books. You can group students by genre types.

Activity 48—Panel Discussion on a Book

Name: _____ Date: _____

Title: _____

Author: _____

Publisher and year: _____

Directions: Each group member is responsible for participating in a panel discussion on the book you read. Group members will sit together, but each person will pull a question from a hat to answer individually. At the end of the question/answer time, the groups will be given time to write down what they learned from the day.

Members of Panel:

1. _____   3. _____

2. _____   4. _____

Write down the question pulled for each member in the group:

1. _____

2. _____

3. _____

4. _____

After discussion, write what you learned:

1. _____

2. _____

3. _____

4. _____

Activity 49—Radio/Television Commercial

Purpose of the Activity

This speaking/listening activity allows students to be highly creative in our media-centered world and to learn about advertisement. The students will experience the process of producing a concise radio commercial segment or a television commercial. The students can work cooperatively. Depending on the age level, they might research examples of professionally made radio or television spots. They can record observations from local radio or television commercials. Finally, students are responsible for creating a product for listening or viewing in class.

How to Use the Activity

The availability of equipment at students' homes or school, such as tape recorders and video recorders, will be a deciding factor in assigning this type of activity for all students. It can be offered as one of several projects from this book. Before this activity is assigned, students need to discuss advertisements and what elements they have in common such as content, appeal, timing, and appearance. Samples can be played in class as models. I have written to companies requesting a radio spot that I heard on the radio. I have received the actual commercials on tape. The companies do not charge a fee if used for educational purposes.

If book promotion is unfamiliar to students, movie advertisements and book advertisements from the newspapers can be talked about and viewed as well. Another pre-project activity for students is having them listen to a radio so they become aware of the use of voices, sound effects, and timing. Many young people are unfamiliar with this genre and enjoy it. Make sure that some class time is allowed for organization, planning, and practice. If your school has a media specialist, his or her assistance and expertise could ensure greater success of the project.

Evaluation

The students can be evaluated by the criteria requested by you for this project. The class can also partake in the evaluation by discussing the strengths and weaknesses of the presentations or by writing comments for each commercial.

Variations

The students can work in pairs or groups to promote reading using the above formats or with photography. Photographs of students reading their favorite book from the class could be enlarged and hung as posters for both reading and book promotion. It is also helpful for students to see adults model reading and writing, so the project could be expanded to include adult role models from home or in school.

Activity 49—Radio/Television Commercial

Name: _____ Date: _____

Title: _____

Author: _____

Publisher and year: _____

Directions: Just as television shows and movies advertise their products, books need advertising too. You are to create a radio spot on a cassette tape or a television spot on videotape to promote your book. Because advertising time is expensive, your commercial can be no longer than one minute. Your spot must be well planned and well rehearsed before taping.

Here is a list of points you might include:

1. Make sure to give accurate information about the book.
2. Tell what kind of book it is so readers know how to locate it in a bookstore or library.
3. Say who would be interested in reading it.
4. Give reasons why someone would want to read the book.
5. Possibly read a short paragraph of interest.
6. Interview someone who has read the book and liked it.
7. If you are doing a TV spot, then the speaker and background are important for the audience.
8. Make sure to time the commercial and listen to it for errors.
9. Use background music only if it is not distracting.
10. Perform the project live in front of the class audience, but it will only have one take.

Remember to Practice, Practice, and Practice!

Activity 50—Live Interview

Purpose of the Activity

This activity has several purposes, and it emphasizes the reading, writing, speaking, and listening standards. Students will read a work of literature in order to express their opinions, feelings, and interpretations of it. Students will work in pairs or groups of three or four, cooperatively writing questions to conduct interviews with each other. The standard of speaking is reinforced through the interview presentations, which are practiced and then performed in front of the class. The students in the class will learn how their classmates feel, interpret, or think about a book, thus practicing their listening skills throughout the presentations.

How to Use the Activity

This activity can be used with a class book or with individual books. You must decide if the interviews are to be in pairs or in groups for larger classes. A discussion on the process of interviewing should take place when this activity begins because not all students may be aware of the need to write open-ended questions that provoke responses other than yes or no. The questions should be short and the responses long. The interviewer needs to practice nodding, listening, and asking follow-up questions of the interviewee. Even though the interviews are rehearsed, the students will do the presentations in a live setting. The activity sheet can be used in the preparation stage and approved by the teacher before the live interview takes place. Each student can use the same questions for each pair or group.

Evaluation

The activity can be evaluated as a formal presentation in which the entire process is taken into consideration, including preparation time, cooperation with peers, and the speaking presentation of the interview. The audience can be assessed for their behavior and listening skills.

Variations

A variation for this activity that would add spontaneity and make the presentations more impromptu would be to ask the interviewer-interviewee groups to write questions that they can ask other groups. This would eliminate rehearsal time, so the responses would be less well thought out but more natural. Another possibility is for each group to have just one interviewer, with all other students in the group as interviewees. You must set the time limitations and the amount of questioning to be done. This project can be offered as one of several possibilities for students to choose from for a book presentation.

Activity 50—Live Interview

Name: _____ Date: _____

Title: _____

Author: _____

Publisher and year: _____

Directions: Present an interview of one or two people who have read a book. The interview needs to be well-planned and practiced. The questions should be carefully written so the audience learns important information about the book.

Interviewer: _____ Interviewee: _____

Question 1

Question 2

Question 3

Question 4

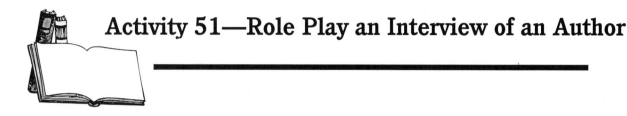

Activity 51—Role Play an Interview of an Author

Purpose of the Activity

This speaking/listening activity has several purposes. First, the students will learn the interviewing process by cooperatively researching, preparing, writing, practicing, and presenting an interview for the class. Second, the students will learn more about the author and the work of literature as they discuss, research, and write questions and answers for the interview. Third, the students will play the roles of interviewer and author. Fourth, the students practice their speaking skills by presenting the interview to the class, while the class practices their listening and audience skills. Fifth, the students use higher-level thinking skills by drawing conclusions for the class based on the information presented.

How to Use the Activity

This activity would work well with a class book or several independent books. Students may work in pairs, either assigned or matched because they are reading the same title or author. Students need to be aware of interview techniques, questioning, and responding. Brainstorming or mapping can be used to find out about their prior knowledge of the process. A taped interview can be viewed in class or watched on television as homework. Give class time for students to plan, discuss, and research the project. You can set the parameters for questions, length, and depth. The author's biography and picture can be obtained by contacting the publisher or checking with the library and on the Internet.

Evaluation

This project can be assessed as a formal presentation for both individuals. The factors to consider for students are meeting a deadline, being prepared, following directions, having accurate content, using good speaking skills, staying in the role assigned, and informing the class about the book and author through their choice of questions and answers.

Variations

You can provide materials for research for younger children. As an entire class project, the students could each be assigned a particular author, or they could randomly draw names of authors of books that were already read in class.

Activity 51—Role Play an Interview of an Author

Name: _____ Date:_____

Title: _____

Author: _____

Publisher and year: _____

Directions: You and a partner will work together to find out information about the author of your book. You and your partner will write questions for a pretend interview of the author. Then you will write pretend responses that both of you believe the author would think. Try to base the responses on the information that you found.

Possible topics: personal life, purpose for writing, other titles, where he/she lives, hobbies, how he/she became a writer

Interviewer:_____ Pretend Author:_____

Question 1 **Response**

Question 2 **Response**

Question 3

Response

Question 4

Response

Question 5

Response

Question 6

Response

Activity 52—Dramatize a Scene

Purpose of the Activity

This speaking/listening activity gives students the opportunity to use their acting and speaking talents. Students must choose an appropriate scene that displays characterization, moves the plot forward, or shows insight. They must work together to plan, organize, rehearse, and perform the scene in the classroom. This project is designed so that students whose learning style is one of action and words will succeed with this form of book project. The members of the class must practice acceptable behavior and active listening skills. The students will learn from each other about the work of literature by hearing the text and dialogue out loud.

How to Use the Activity

To avoid rewriting, students need to choose scenes that contain a great deal of dialogue and very little narration. If you want all your students to act and speak in front of an audience, the class can be divided into groups, and several scenes can be presented. This activity can be offered as one of several choices from this book. The activity sheet can be used to help students organize themselves in the planning stages and can be collected for approval. You will set the time limits for the presentations.

Evaluations

The students can be evaluated in several ways. The total assessment can include the planning sheet, a rough draft of the scene with the parts labeled, how well the students work together, and the final performance. The audience behavior can be assessed as well.

Variations

One variation might be to ask students to change the genre of the story into another form such as a poem, play, short story, or screenplay.

Activity 52—Dramatize a Scene

Name: _____ Date: _____

Title: _____

Author: _____

Publisher and year: _____

Directions: Work in groups and act out a scene from your book that deals with a character's problem, a character's decision, an important action, or a favorite part of the book.

Group Members:

Name of scene and page number: _____

How is this scene important in the book? _____

_____

What were your reasons for choosing this scene?_____

_____

Narrator to fill in information: _____

Characters and description:

1. _____

2. _____

3. _____

Short summary of the scene to be acted: _____

_____

List props, sets, or costumes needed:_____

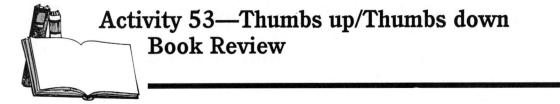

Activity 53—Thumbs up/Thumbs down Book Review

Purpose of Activity

This higher-level thinking activity involves both speaking and listening standards. Students must make judgments on several elements of the book and discuss them with the class. They must form opinions and support them with specific examples from the text. Younger students learn that it is acceptable to have likes and dislikes about a book and that their opinions are important, especially when supported with facts and examples. Students will also practice their speaking skills with an audience while the audience practices listening to their peers' opinions and deciding if they agree or disagree.

How to Use the Activity

This activity can be used with students reading a variety of selections so students can listen to the book reviews and decide which books they would like to read. If all the students have read the same book, they can listen to their classmates' opinions on it. The students can discuss what kinds of elements should be considered for the book reviews. For younger children, you can be more directive with specific points to evaluate. Sample book or movie reviews can be used as examples to build students' prior knowledge. Time can be given in class for students to find examples from the text to support their opinions. The time limitation for the presentation should be stated at the onset on the project.

Evaluation

This formal presentation can be assessed according to the presentation of judgments about elements of the book with adequate support from the text. For younger children, choose topics such as characters, pictures, difficulty of words, likes or dislikes, and the story line of the plot. Speaking skills, meeting a deadline, organization, and knowledge of the text are other factors to consider. The audience can also be assessed for listening skills.

Variations

You can require a visual chart of the information being presented for students to get used to handling a visual aid. The posters can be hung around the room for students to view throughout the week. A writing suggestion is to ask students to write an overall summary of what was learned.

Activity 53—Thumbs up/Thumbs down Book Review

Name: _____ Date:_____

Title: _____

Author: _____

Publisher and year: _____

Directions: Give a short book review on 3 areas of the book such as characters, plot, problem/solution, suspense, held your interest, or other points. Use a "thumbs up" for positive (like), and a "thumbs down" for negative (dislike). Make sure you explain your reasons (Why?) with examples from the book.

Element of Book Being Critiqued	👍 👎	Why?
1.	👍 👎	
2.	👍 👎	
3.	👍 👎	

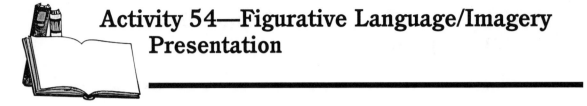

Activity 54—Figurative Language/Imagery Presentation

Purpose of the Activity

The primary purpose of this activity is for students to show their understanding of figurative language and imagery as used by an author. Students must understand the terms and look for examples from the text in order to share lines, passages, and interpretations with their peers. The students will practice their speaking skills, and the class will practice listening skills by participating as an audience.

How to Use the Activity

This activity can be used with an entire class, or it can be offered as one of several choices from this book. The literary terms should be taught, modeled, and practiced, possibly with poetry, before this activity is assigned with a book. Students need to become familiar with these writing devices before they can look for them in a larger work. The worksheet can be used as a rough draft before a presentation. For the lower grades, you might want to assign only three boxes and with the older grades, such as third through sixth, you might want to assign all of the boxes. By having students read their findings aloud, the whole class hears the author's picturesque language. Students can work in pairs to help each other figure out the literal meanings of the figurative language.

Evaluation

Depending on your purpose, this activity can be assessed as a class assignment or as a formal presentation. If it is used as a formal presentation, students must practice the words from the text and their explanations for the meanings of the quotes before their presentations. Speaking skills such as eye contact, clarity, articulation, enunciation, and volume are all important parts of a presentation.

Variations

Students can use this activity to practice writing their own stylistic devices. These devices can be used in future writing assignments. Another possibility is for students to look for writing devices in newspapers and magazines. You can place poster paper on the wall and have the students paste the examples of figurative language and imagery on the poster after they share with the class.

Activity 54—Figurative Language/Imagery Presentation

Name: _____ Date:_____

Title: _____

Author: _____

Publisher and year: _____

Directions: This activity is a search for specific forms of imagery and figurative language that the author used in his/her book to create word pictures and word descriptions.

Find one example from your book of _____ different kinds of this special kind of writing. Make sure you write down the page number. Then explain the meaning of the expression.

Be prepared to share a sample with the class.

Simile—A comparison using "like" or "as"   (She is as sweet as honey.)

Metaphor—A comparison not using "like" or "as"   (She is a honey.)

Personification—Giving human traits to nonliving objects
(the hands of a clock)

Hyperbole—An exaggeration
(I am so hungry that I could eat a horse.)

Onomatopoeia—Words that resemble the sounds
(Snap, crackle, pop!)

Imagery—Words that create "visual" word pictures
(I see the thick, leafy, green branches.)

Imagery—Words that create "sound" word pictures
(I can hear the dripping water plop on the deck.)

Imagery—Words that create "taste" word pictures
(The popcorn tasted buttery, crunchy, and salty.)

Imagery—Words that create "touch" word pictures
(The peach felt soft, round, and fuzzy.)

Imagery—Words that create "smell" word pictures
(The kitchen smelled of pizza, garlic, and many spices.)

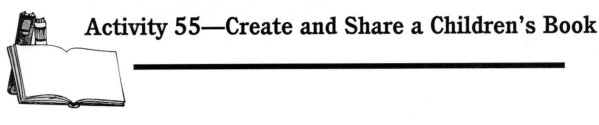

Activity 55—Create and Share a Children's Book

Purpose of the Activity

This activity combines all the standards of reading, writing, representing, viewing, speaking, and listening. First, the students will read a book and understand the plot and the point of the book. Secondly, they must show their understanding of the book and of the parts of a story by writing their own children's book containing similar characters, plot, and theme by rewriting it for a younger audience. Thirdly, they will represent the meaning of each chapter by a page in a picture book illustrated with personal drawings. Fourthly, they will share their books with their class or a younger class by reading aloud and practicing fluency skills. Fifth, the audience will practice listening skills and gain a greater understanding of universal themes and the elements of fictional stories.

How to Use the Activity

This activity can be assigned to all members of a class, or it can be offered as one of several choices after a book is finished. Before this project is assigned, students should read several children's books to learn the format of the genre as well as the plot, characters, setting, mood, and theme (especially for older children). After evaluating the qualities of a good book, they need to find these elements in the books they read. Younger children can draw a picture of their favorite scene in the book and write about it. Older children can experience the process of pre-writing, planning, drafting, revising, re-writing, editing, and producing a final draft. Students learn about the difficult process of illustrating a book in a way that will convey the same meaning as the words.

Evaluation

This formal project can be assessed according to all standards listed above. The students should be told the assessment process at the onset of the project, especially any areas that you want them to concentrate on more heavily.

Variations

Offer the students the opportunity to read their stories not only to their peers but also to lower elementary students or preschool students. Older students take pride in their work if it is appreciated in a real setting.

Activity 55—Create and Share a Children's Book

Name: _____ Date: _____

Title: _____

Author: _____

Publisher and year: _____

Directions: Create a children's picture book to share with younger children similar to the one you have just finished reading. Use the form on the next page to design and lay out the book. The four squares below can help you plan your ideas.

You are assigned to do _____ pages for your book.

The top part of the sheet should be used for an illustration (picture) and the bottom part should be used for text (written words).

Be prepared to read your book aloud on _____ .

Activity 56—Poem Made from the Title of Your Book

Purpose of the Activity

This activity involves writing, speaking, and listening standards. Students will write a creative poem based on the title of a work of literature. Older students can learn what an acrostic poem is. They will show their own meanings and feelings through their interpretation. The students must also illustrate the ideas of the poem which will give another opportunity to communicate through symbols. The students will share their own poem aloud with the class. Afterward, to increase the students' self-esteem, the poems can be displayed in the classroom either on a bulletin board or as a booklet containing the entire class's poems. The booklets can be photocopied, stapled, and given to each class member.

How to Use the Activity

Because the formula for writing an acrostic poem is simple, all students can be successful at this fun activity. It can be used for a class book or individual books, and it can be used as a class activity rather than a take-home assignment. Students can create their poems by hand or on a computer. Sharing can be either formally in front of the class or informally in a circle. You must decide on the purpose of the activity and make the students aware of its value. For younger children who may not have many words in their background knowledge from which to choose, ask them to write either a free verse poem of three to five lines or have words on a prepared sheet that begin with the letters of the words in the title. Students can then choose from the selection and still do an acrostic poem if the title is not too long.

Evaluation

This activity can be assessed as a class activity, homework assignment, or book project depending on the level, age, and maturity of the children. You may want to give credit for the sharing and publishing portion of the activity if special emphasis is placed on it during the learning process.

Variations

Students also enjoy making acrostics out of their names, cities, characters' names, vocabulary, and other significant words to them. This form of poetry can be used as an introduction to a poetry unit. Sometimes this kind of poetry is useful as a memory cue for remembering words or details.

Activity 56—Poem Made from the Title of Your Book

Name: _____ Date:_____

Title: _____

Author: _____

Publisher and year: _____

Directions:
- You are to write a poem using the beginning letters of the words from the title of your book.
- The poem does not rhyme.
- The title of the book is written in a vertical line.
- Each letter begins a new line.
- Each line may be a word, phrase, or sentence.
- Illustrations (pictures) around the poem will make it attractive.
- The words you use should be about your feelings or main ideas from the book.
- Everyone will read their poem out loud to the class and will show their drawings.

This
Is
The
Lovely
Example

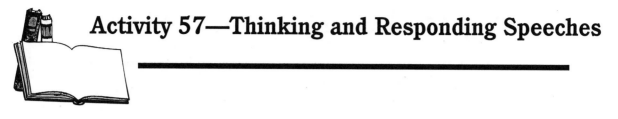

Activity 57—Thinking and Responding Speeches

Purpose of the Activity

This speaking/listening activity gives students the opportunity to practice thinking in a short amount of time, a necessary life skill. Students must organize their thoughts quickly to present a short response based on a just-completed book. They must use specific examples from the reading to support their opinions. Finally, they will practice their speaking skills in front of an audience while the audience practices listening skills.

How to Use the Activity

This class activity is most successful after a book has been read, either by the class or by individuals. The response questions should be cut up and placed in a container so students can randomly draw one to respond to in an impromptu speech to your specified length of time. The speeches can be timed so that all students have the opportunity to speak in the same class period. Either before or after the speeches, you can discuss the necessity of learning the useful life skill of thinking on one's feet quickly. You can even brainstorm with the children the jobs and places in the world that this skill is important. (There is a reproducible brainstorming sheet on page 32.)

Evaluation

This activity can be assessed in terms of participation, answering the chosen response, and speaking skills. The amount of credit for the activity depends on your purpose and the level of the class. One possibility is simply to give students "A" for completing the response presentation or "0" for choosing not to participate. I find that almost every time I use this type of grading, every student chooses to participate and the pressure of the grade is removed from the anxiety of speaking.

Variations

Students can write their own questions that they would like answered about the book, and impromptu speeches can be used with any type of literature or even nonfiction.

Activity 57—Thinking and Responding Speeches

Name: _____ Date: _____

Title: _____

Author: _____

Publisher and year: _____

Directions: Pick from a bag a question about the book you just read. You will have a short amount of time to think and one minute to answer the question. Try to use specific examples in your response.

Questions in the bag:

1. What does the title mean?

2. What came as a surprise to you in the book and why?

3. Are you like any of the characters? Explain.

4. What was the best part of the book and why?

5. Who should read this book and why?

6. Was there a character that reminds you of a real person you know? Explain.

7. Did you like the ending of the book? Why or why not?

8. What do you predict will happen after the ending? Explain.

9. What character would you like to be and why?

10. Is there a character that you would like to have as a friend and why?

11. What confused you in the book?

12. What are five words that would describe the main character?

13. Was there a person who could be considered a hero for some reason and why?

14. What was the problem in the book? What was the solution to the problem?

15. What feeling did you have when you were reading? What happened to make you feel this way?

16. What part did you dislike in the book and why?

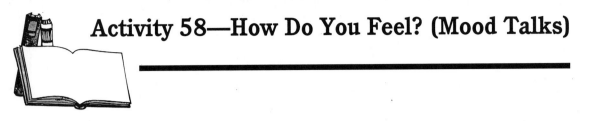

Activity 58—How Do You Feel? (Mood Talks)

Purpose of the Activity

This speaking and listening activity has students speak in front of their classmates after being given only a short time to prepare. This forces students to think quickly, form opinions, organize what they will say, and support their opinions with examples from the text. The students must analyze the emotions of a character in a book in various situations. Then the students must think about their own feelings while reading their books. The class members will practice listening skills and audience behavior. By choosing common emotions, the speakers reinforce their knowledge about the mood created by the author to get the readers emotionally involved in the text. Also the children learn that people are similar in the emotions they experience.

How to Use the Activity

This activity would be most successful as a post-reading activity. Students enjoy randomly drawing their assignments rather than having specific ones, so cut the chart into pieces and put them into a box or hat. You can also have them draw numbers to determine the order of their presentations. After students draw their slips of paper, you can decide how long they have to prepare their speeches and how many examples should be given from the text by using the brainstorming sheet (page 32) in this book. Students may need to look in the text for support for the responses. A good time limit for the presentations is one minute each.

Evaluation

This speaking activity can be assessed as other speeches have been. Students should be aware from the beginning what the evaluation process will include. Speaking elements such as clarity, volume, pacing, and eye contact can be factors in the evaluation. The audience can be evaluated in terms of attentiveness and appropriate behavior.

Variations

This activity can be used to teach or review moods with any kind of literature. Whenever an activity can be made into a game, the students are more eager to participate and the chances for success increase. In this vein, have students think of situations from one or several books and write them down on cards. Then randomly draw the cards and ask the students to match them with the emotions and feelings on the sheet. The first student to get a predetermined number of matches correct is the winner and receives extra points.

Activity 58—How Do You Feel? (Mood Talks)

Name: _____ Date: _____

Title: _____

Author: _____

Publisher and year: _____

Directions:
- First, think of a character from your book.
- Then, think about his/her feelings or emotions that were shown during the story.
- Next, think about how you felt at the beginning, middle, or end of the book.
- You will share your ideas with others.

Happiness	Sadness	Excitement	Anger
Suspense	Confusion	Jealousy	Disappointment
Depression	Frustration	Relief	Stress
Determination	Exhaustion	Surprise	Shock
Ashamed	Embarrassed	Frightened	Naughty
Lonely	Guilty	Proud	Helpful

Activity 59—Create a Game

Purpose of the Activity

Although this activity involves some writing skills, the emphasis is on speaking and listening skills and cooperative learning. Students must work together to create one or all of the games—Jeopardy, Wheel of Fortune, or a board game—based on aspects of a book. They must not only design the game's format but also create the rules, questions, answers, and ways of winning. Then they will share their game with the class or other groups and play it. Students will learn from each other as they discuss various aspects of a book, such as vocabulary, characters, plot, themes, setting, or other topics suggested by you or the class. This activity can be used as a review and post-reading activity. Students take turns reading and asking the questions. The other students can practice listening skills as they participate.

How to Use the Activity

Students can be divided into groups so that all members are working on the same project at the same time but creating different games. Another possibility is to offer this project as one of several choices so that students interested in this creative endeavor can undertake this project. If all students are working on group games, then groups may want to take turns playing each other's creations. The games should be simple enough for all class members to play, yet contain informational elements so that they are learning devices. Before game creation starts, discuss the students' favorite games and what elements are necessary for a good group or board game. Because students are often more familiar with computer games than board games, board games could be brought into the classroom to display the board, directions, pieces, and accessories. Students can use poster board to replicate and enlarge the board games or the Wheel of Fortune "wheels." The prizes can be pencils, stickers, one night of "no homework," or extra credit points on their grade.

Evaluation

This project can be assessed as a creative project would be in terms of meeting a deadline, originality, creativity, information, organization, and practicality. The students can be evaluated on their cooperative working and their game-playing participation. The game playing points can be counted however you feel you would like to assess.

Variations

You can control the type of game to be created and the topics that the games cover. You could involve several book titles and several authors depending on the age of the children.

Activity 59—Create a Game

Name: _____ Date: _____

Title: _____

Author: _____

Publisher and year: _____

Jeopardy Directions:

You are to write 3 answers/questions under specific categories relating to your book. Then there will be teams, and we will follow the Jeopardy rules for points and prizes.

Possible Categories: (Circle the ones chosen to use)

Characters	Setting	Vocabulary
Related Books	Author Information	Themes
Details	Plot	Foreshadowing

Answers and Questions

1. _____

Question: _____

2. _____

Question: _____

3. _____

Question: _____

Wheel of Fortune Directions:

You are to write 5 important words or phrases from your book and then write a clue or the related category. We will design a wheel and form teams to play the game.

- -

Word or phrase 1:_____

Clue or category 1:_____

- -

Word or phrase 2: _____

Clue or category 2:_____

- -

Word or phrase 3: _____

Clue or category 3:_____

- -

Word or phrase 4: _____

Clue or category 4: _____

- -

Word or phrase 5: _____

Clue or category 5: _____

- -

Board Game Directions:

You will work with a team to create a board game based on aspects of your book. You must be accurate and write directions for your game. Use the form below for your rough draft.

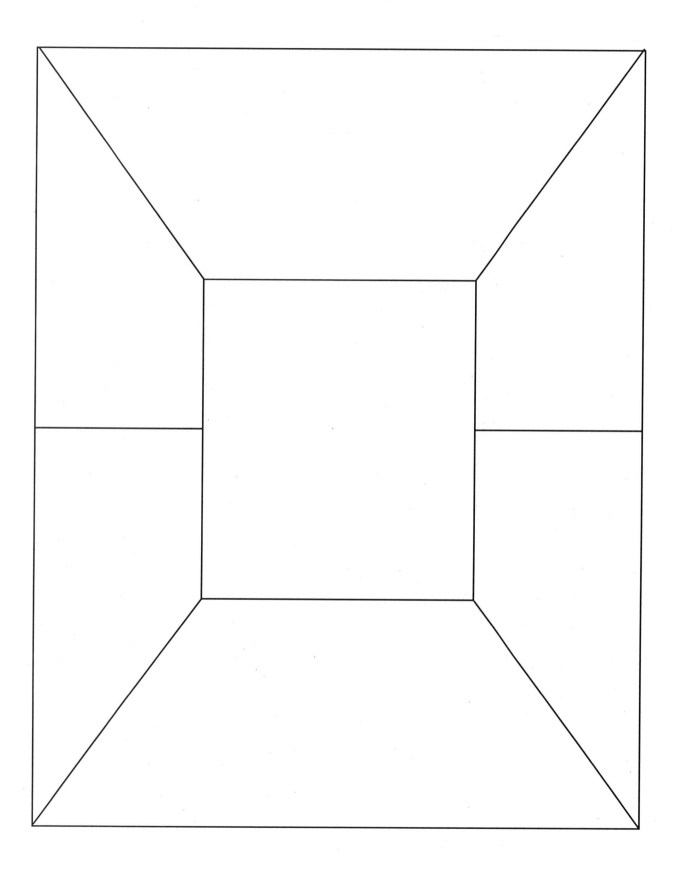

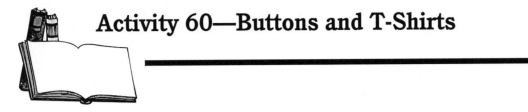

Activity 60—Buttons and T-Shirts

Purpose of the Activity

There are several purposes for this activity. The first is to have students think, write, and create nontraditional communication forms such as message buttons and T-shirts, which can contain important universal messages. Secondly, the students will promote both their books and the pleasure of reading. Thirdly, by having the students present their button and T-shirt designs to the class along with an explanation for their creations, they can be proud of their work. Fourth, the audience will practice listening skills.

How to Use the Activity

This activity can be done by an entire class or given as one of several projects for students to choose from for their project and presentation. Discuss the ideas of universal themes and marketing approaches used when trying to promote a project. Several examples of buttons, T-shirts, cups, magnets, and other promotional items can be brought in as examples. Because space is limited, word choice and catchy sayings become significant. Artwork, color, and design are issues that an art teacher can speak to the class about or that can be researched.

There are two buttons on the activity page; one is to promote the book, and the other is to promote the idea of reading for enjoyment. The T-shirt design can be enlarged for more effect. After students present the projects to the class, the items can be displayed as magnets in the classroom.

Evaluation

This activity can be assessed informally or formally depending on whether it is a class activity or a formal book project. Originality, creativity, appearance, message content, and explanation of the message in relationship to the book are all factors to consider. Students in the audience will be graded on listening skills and appropriate audience behavior.

Variations

Once the buttons and T-shirts are created, you can laminate them for safekeeping. Students can draw or create on a computer many other objects that can be used for promotion, such as hats, belts, candy bars, kites, or billboards. Attaching magnetic strips to the back of any of these objects makes them useful messages for refrigerators.

Activity 60—Buttons and T-Shirts

Name: _____ Date: _____

Title: _____

Author: _____

Publisher and year: _____

Directions: Brainstorm possible messages, sayings, and things that you learned after reading your book. Also, brainstorm ways to promote reading for others. Then narrow your choices to create two buttons. One button must refer to your book and the other to reading in general.

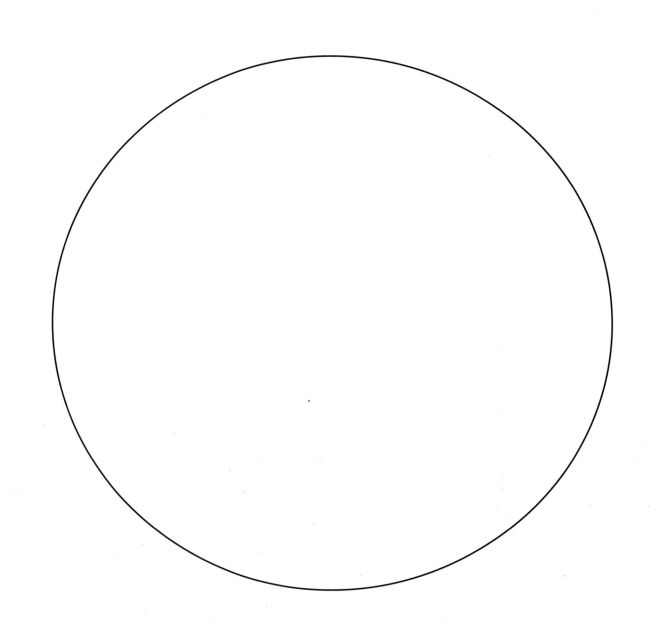

Directions: Many times T-shirts are used for a message or advertisement. Design a T-shirt to promote either your book or the pleasure of reading.

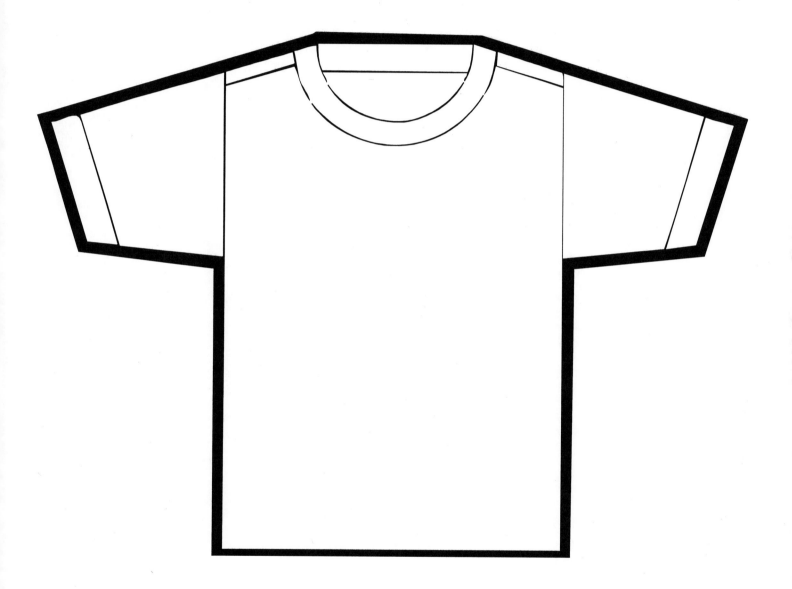

FROM TEACHER IDEAS PRESS

STARTING WITH SHAKESPEARE: Successfully Introducing Shakespeare to Children
Pauline Nelson and Todd Daubert

William Shakespeare comes alive for students with these engaging activities. This book introduces elementary students to four plays—"A Midsummer Night's Dream," "Macbeth," "Hamlet," and "Romeo and Juliet." A complete historical background, an introduction to the characters, a retelling of the story, a variety of integrated activities, verses for memorization, a complete script for class performance, and a list of resources accompany each play. **Grades K–5 (adaptable to higher levels).**
xv, 217p. 8½x11 paper ISBN 1-56308-753-7

BRIDGES TO READING, K–3 AND 3–6: Teaching Reading Skills with Children's Literature
Suzanne I. Barchers

These resources reconcile the need to teach basic skills with the desire to use children's literature. They include stimulating and instructive lessons based on approximately 150 skills commonly found in basal readers. Semantic feature analysis, attribute charts, writing activities, problem-solving, genre analysis, wordplay, and phonetic analysis are just some of the strategies covered.
Grades K–3: *ix, 201p. 8½x11 paper ISBN 1-56308-758-8*
Grades 3–6: *vii, 179p. 8 1/2x11 paper ISBN 1-56308-759-6*

SUPER SIMPLE STORYTELLING: A Can-Do Guide for Every Classroom, Every Day
Kendall Haven

This book has everything you need to get started, including detailed directions and guides for more than 40 powerful storytelling exercises to use with your class. You'll find the Golden List of what an audience really needs from storytelling, a proven, step-by-step system for successfully learning and remembering a story, the Great-Amazing-Never-Fail Safety Net to prevent storytelling disasters, and more. **All Levels.**
xxvii, 229p. 8½x11 paper ISBN 1-56308-681-6

MULTICULTURAL FOLKTALES: Readers Theatre for Elementary Students
Suzanne I. Barchers

Introduce your students to other countries and cultures through the traditional folk and fairy tales in these engaging readers theatre scripts. Representing more than 30 countries and regions, the 40 reproducible scripts are accompanied by presentation suggestions and recommendations for props and delivery. **Grades 1–5.**
xxi, 188p. 8½x11 paper ISBN 1-56308-760-X

WHAT A NOVEL IDEA! Projects and Activities for Young Adult Literature
Katherine Wiesolek Kuta

Like *Novel Ideas for Young Readers* but geared to teens, each of the 60 reproducible classroom-ready activities has general guidelines that describe the purposes for the project, how to use it, evaluation points, and variations that increase student participation and motivation, and a variety of assessment activities. **Grades 6–12.**
xi, 143p. 8½x11 paper ISBN 1-56308-479-1

For a free catalog or to place an order, please contact Teacher Ideas Press.
•Phone: 800-237-6124 • Fax: 303-220-8843 • Visit: www.lu.com
•Mail to: Dept. B042 • P.O. Box 6633 • Englewood, CO 80155-6633